Introducti

On the coast, adjoining the Menai St from Anglesey (Ynys Mon), are two ir One is the small cathedral and unive other is Caernarfon, a fortified walled town of Roman origins, with an impressive late 13thC castle, and now a designated World Heritage Site. During the 19thC both places, along with Port Dinorwic lying between the two, became important slate ports serving vast inland quarries at a time when North West Wales was the main producer of slate in the world, and the slate industry dominated the local economy. Huge quantities of slate were shipped to meet the demand for roofing tiles in the rapidly developing industrial towns in Britain and elsewhere.

The old quarries and small communities that developed near them, lie at the edge of the Snowdonia National Park. Bethesda, the largest, grew alongside Penrhyn quarry which became the world's biggest open cast slate quarry, and from where slate went by rail to Port Penrhyn in Bangor. Caernarfon was the port for the quarries of the Nantlle valley and Moel Tryfan area. The industrial legacy includes old quarries (some water-filled), former tramways, a network of quarrymen's paths and the trackbed of former narrow gauge railways used to transport the slate.

The 22 walks in this book explore the area's varied landscape and fascinating history. There are town trails, walks by the Menai Strait, through woodland and river valleys, across foothills offering panoramic views, past quarries and through a complex pattern of enclosed fields. Some follow old miners' paths and sections of former railways, now surfaced recreational trails such as Lôn Las Ogwen and Lôn Eifion, the latter offering close views of the steam hauled narrow gauge Welsh Highland Railway. There are good views of Snowdon and other mountains.

The routes follow public rights of way, permissive paths or cross Open Access land, and are within the capability of most people. A key feature is that many routes, as well as containing shorter walk options, can easily be linked with others, to provide longer day walks, if required. Walking boots are recommended, along with appropriate clothing to protect against the elements. Be properly prepared and equipped, especially on the higher routes, where the weather can quickly change. Please remember that path conditions can vary according to season and weather. Contact Gwynedd Council regarding any rights of way problems encountered.

Each walk has a detailed map and description but bear in mind that changes in detail can occur at any time. The location of each walk is shown on the back cover and a summary of their key features is also given. This includes an estimated walking time, but allow more time to enjoy the scenery and sights.

Please observe the country code. *Enjoy your walking!*

WALK 1
BANGOR

DESCRIPTION A varied 3 mile walk exploring Bangor, visiting its main places of interest, including its cathedral, university, green open spaces, and its splendid Victorian pier. Allow about 2 hours.

START Beach Road long stay car park, A5 Bangor [SH 587727] or Clock Tower, High Street [SH 583721].

DIRECTIONS The signposted shoreline car park adjoins the A5 near Kwik-fit on the eastern side of Bangor.

Bangor's origins began with the building of a small church here about 525 AD by St Deiniol, a Celtic missionary. It was enclosed by a interwoven wooden fence, known locally as 'bangor' – a name which became associated with the monastic settlement that developed around the church. In 546 St Deiniol became a bishop and the church a cathedral. The cathedral has survived acts of destruction, making it Britain's oldest in continuous use. The present building dates mainly from the 13th and 14thC, and was extensively restored in 1870-80. In the late 18thC Bangor consisted of a small ecclesiastical community clustered around the cathedral. However the arrival of the turnpike road from Conwy to Caernarfon, with daily coach services from Chester to Holyhead, and the development during the 19thC of Bangor as an important slate port linked by rail to Penrhyn Quarry in Bethesda, saw the city grow in importance. The arrival of the Chester–Holyhead railway in 1848 sustained this growth. In 1884 a University was established and now attracts students from the UK. and around the world.

1 Go through barriers and use the nearby Pelican Crossing to cross the main road to go along Ambrose Street opposite. At its end bend LEFT along Friar's Road then at the junction turn RIGHT along the High Street – said to be the longest in Wales and the UK. At the next junction continue ahead along the no through road through the busy shopping area, soon pedestrianised.

2 At the Victorian clock tower bear RIGHT down the wide pedestrian area between Deiniol and Menai shopping precincts – *with University Top College prominent on the skyline* – towards the bus terminus. At Subway turn LEFT along the pavement then on the bend by the Museum/Art Gallery take the pathway towards the nearby cathedral. Go up its left fork to enter the cathedral by a side door and after looking round leave by the opposite door. Now take a pathway almost opposite down the edge of Bible Garden. At a wide pathway T-junction, turn LEFT, soon passing a car park and war memorial. Cross the main road by the Pelican Crossing and go past Memorial Arch and up the side of Pontio, a new Arts and Innovation Centre due for opening in 2013. Turn RIGHT briefly up a narrow road, then LEFT up a wide walled stepped path through mature trees to a car park. Turn RIGHT, then LEFT up a narrow lane. At the road junction turn RIGHT past the entrance to University Top College, containing fine Edwardian buildings.

3 Go down a pathway on the left between a car park and Hen Goleg past the former teacher training college founded in 1858. Angle RIGHT across the road to enter the corner of Ashley Jones Field. A simple route is to follow the surfaced path parallel with the road, then a grass path to join the road at point 4. A more interesting route is to follow the signposted path along the edge of this open green space towards the Menai Strait, soon bearing RIGHT down to a footbridge over a stream. Continue with a path past a small wood, then a stone circle and down to go through a wall gap. Follow the path ahead up through woodland just above the estuary edge. Soon turn sharp RIGHT up another path to the road.

4 Continue briefly along the road edge, then take a signposted path through a stone archway on the right. Follow it up across the wooded slope to emerge onto an open space known as 'Roman Camp'. Go to nearby seats – *offering extensive views along the Menai Strait and south to the mountains of Snowdonia*. Follow a path down through trees, past a path on the right, to a

WALK I

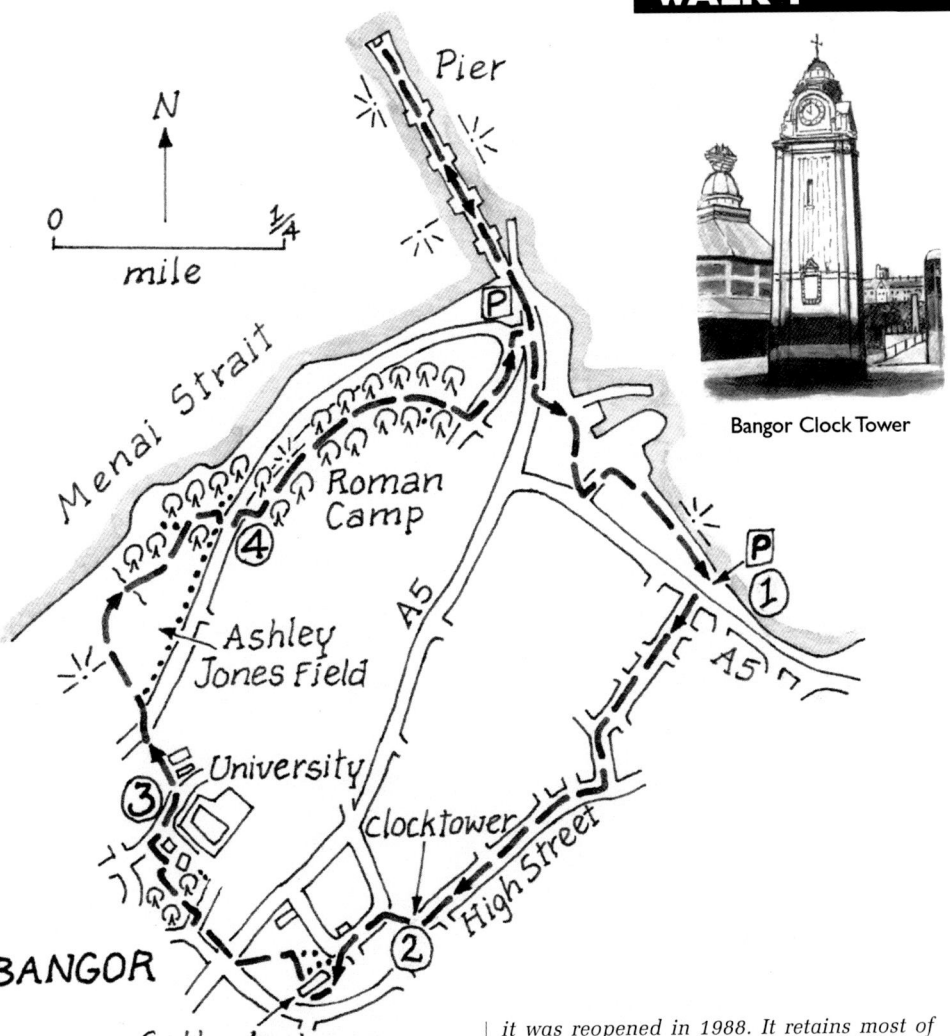

Bangor Clock Tower

small gate and on down between houses to a road. Follow it LEFT then at the junction with Siliwen Road turn RIGHT. At the Tap & Spile pub turn LEFT to the entrance to the pier (a small charge). *The impressive grade 2 listed pier, the second longest in Wales, was built in 1896. Originally 1550 feet in length (now 1500 feet) it included a pontoon landing stage for steamers from the Isle of Man, Blackpool and Liverpool. After falling into disrepair it was closed in 1971 and threatened with demolition. Fortunately, after a public campaign and major restoration work,* *it was reopened in 1988. It retains most of its original features, including its kiosks. It offers superb views along the Strait and east along the coast to the Great Orme, and inland to the Carneddau mountains. Worth visiting at its end is Pavilion Tea rooms (open 09.00-16.00,Thur-Sun) famous for its scones.* Return to the junction by the Tap & Spile and continue along the road ahead. Just before the Boatyard Inn turn LEFT down a narrow lane to the shore and on with cycle route 5 along a stony track. Just before the road by a garage do a sharp U-turn LEFT along a lane (still route 5), then follow the wide shoreline promenade to the start.

3

WALK 2
MENAI BRIDGE

DESCRIPTION A short but interesting 1½ mile walk around the small Victorian town of Menai Bridge (Porthaethwy), featuring the attractive woodland of Coed Cyrnol, the tiny Church Island where St Tysilio founded his church in the 7thC, and two impressive historic bridges across the Menai Strait. Allow about 1 hour.
START Coed Cyrnol car park, Menai Bridge [SH 555719].
DIRECTIONS From Bangor follow the A5 across the Menai Suspension Bridge and over a roundabout. The car park is on the left just beyond the police station.

*T*he Menai Strait is a narrow stretch of water separating Anglesey from the mainland. Its complex strong surging tides, rocks and swirling waters, especially a stretch known as The Swillies, with whirlpools, has for centuries proved to be difficult to navigate and a danger to shipping. Crossing the Strait was an equally hazardous task. Drovers used to swim their cattle and pigs across and from the 17thC there were ferryboats at this location, later carrying carriages on the London to Holyhead coaching route.

*T*homas Telford, the renowned civil engineer, faced the challenge of building the first bridge across the Strait, as part of work to improve the coaching route, an important link to Ireland. It had to be level enough for heavily laden horse-drawn vehicles and high enough to allowing tall sailing ships to pass underneath. His solution was an impressive suspension bridge, 577 feet long and 100 feet high, supported by limestone pillars – at the time the longest in the world. Work commenced in 1819 and the bridge was opened on the 30th January 1826. Its 16 huge wrought iron chains supporting the roadway, were soaked in linseed oil and later painted to prevent rusting. 150 men were involved in the lifting of the key central section of chain, weighing over 23 tons, by block and tackle. Its successful completion was greeted with much applause from the large crowd that had gathered to watch this major task. The original roadway, offering two narrow single carriageways, was made of wood. The bridge greatly improved the journey time from London to Holyhead and led to the growth of the small town and port of Menai Bridge, with a thriving cattle market. In 1938 the iron chains were replaced with steel ones, due to the increasingly heavy traffic.

*F*urther west along the Strait is the Brittania railway bridge, which was built to carry the Chester-Holyhead railway. It had to be strong enough to carry heavy fast moving trains across a wide span and to facilitate the passing of ships. The solution of Robert Stephenson, the son of George, the famous locomotive engineer, was to build over three years the world's first tubular wrought iron bridge, which opened in 1850. His design revolutionised the use of iron in bridge building. The tubular bridge through which trains ran, was 1,511 feet long and supported by masonry piers. Box sections weighing 1500 tons were assembled on the shore, floated into position then lifted into place. The bridge was decorated with four large limestone lions. After a fire in 1970 the bridge was redesigned to carry both rail and road traffic.

1 From information boards descend steps to the nearby wide pathway and follow it through mature woodland down to a path junction overlooking the Menai Strait. Go across the causeway then follow a path anti-clockwise round the edge of the graveyard – with a good view to Stephenson's bridge – to reach the small 15thC St Tysilio's church. Go through the graveyard and return across the causeway. Turn RIGHT along the Belgian Promenade past information boards to join a lane. Keep ahead, then follow the signposted Coast Path round a small wooded area, before rejoining the road to pass under the massive arches of Telford's suspension bridge to pass a picnic area with an information board.

2 Just beyond a junction go through a gate by toilets and follow the path round the bowling green to a shelter seat in the far corner – offering a good view along the Menai Strait to Bangor Pier. Follow a path below

WALK 2

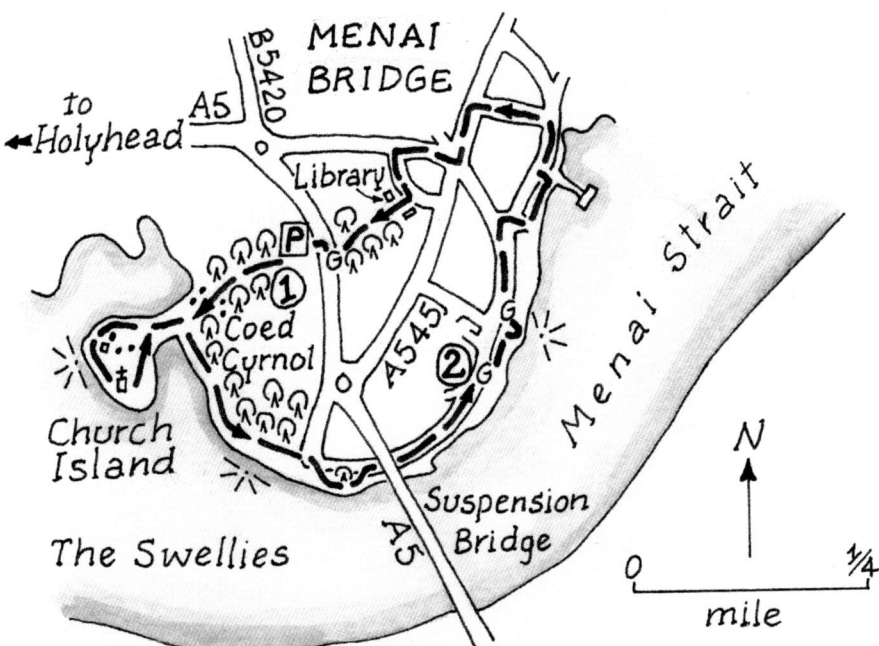

back to the road. Follow it past the slipway, then at the Liverpool Arms turn RIGHT to pass the Pier Gatehouse. Follow the road to St George's pier (1904) – *where paddle-steamers once disembarked visitors from Liverpool* – then continue along StGeorge's Road. Turn LEFT along Askew Street to the High Street. Turn LEFT. At Uxbridge Square turn RIGHT and go along Dale Street. Turn LEFT along Wood Street past the library, then turn RIGHT past Llys y Ffair and go up a signposted path through trees to the main road. Turn RIGHT back to the start.

Menai Suspension Bridge

WALK 3
THE SPINNIES

DESCRIPTION A meandering 6¼ mile figure of eight walk (**A**) from the foreshore of Traeth Lafan to the lower slopes of foothills to the south. The walk, which follows field paths and quiet country roads, features good views of the coast and Penrhyn Castle, with a visit to The Spinnies Nature Reserve to finish. Allow about 3½ hours. A shorter 1¾ mile walk (**B**) is included.

START Aber Ogwen car park [SH 616724].

DIRECTIONS From Bangor, turn off the A5 by the entrance to Penrhyn Castle towards Tal-y-Bont, passing over the river. Ignore turnings into Tal-y-Bont, then take a minor road on the left, signposted 'Nature Reserve' to find the shoreline car park at its end.

*T**raeth Lafan*, a large inter tidal area extending from Bangor to Llanfairfechan, is a Local Nature Reserve of international importance. The sand, shingle, saltmarsh and extensive mudflats exposed at low tide stretching over towards Anglesey, offer an abundance of food – ie. ragworms, snails, cockles, and mussels, as well as fish – that attract and sustain a wide variety of birds, including large numbers of over wintering waders. The sands support the largest population of moulting great crested grebes in Britain. The Spinnies, one of several nature reserves adjoining Traeth Lafan, is managed by the North Wales Wildlife Trust Set amongst small woodland the reserve contains ponds, a reed edged lagoon and two hides for discreet viewing of the many species of birds seen here.

1 From the far end of the car park follow the signposted Coast Path east along the edge of the stony foreshore – *with a view across Traeth Lafan to Beaumaris* – soon rising through trees to a kissing gate. Continue along the fenced path on the low tree-lined cliffs to go through another kissing gate by a small gate. Now head inland along the field edge a ladder-stile/gate by farm buildings – *enjoying a first view west to Penrhyn Castle. The neo-Norman castle, with its huge keep, was built by eminent architect Thomas Hopper in the mid-19th C for Lord Penrhyn. It symbolised the family's power and influence in this part of North Wales, and their considerable wealth made from the profits of Penrhyn slate quarry in Bethesda and slave labour worked sugar plantations in Jamaica.* Go through the farmyard, then a gate ahead. Go along the field edge to a gate and along the next to an iron ladder-stile. Turn RIGHT along the field edge to another ladder-stile in the corner and a stream beyond. Angle LEFT across the middle of the large field to a ladder-stile/gate in a recessed corner by a wood. (For **Walk B**, midway turn right to a kissing gate in the right-hand corner to join the returning main walk.) Follow the green track to nearby gates, under the railway, through a small wood, along a field edge to join a concrete track to reach the road near Tan-y-lon. Turn LEFT along the road verge, over the A55, then at the junction keep ahead past Hendre. The quiet country lane rises steadily alongside a stream, past a house and up more steeply through delightful mature woodland, featuring bluebells in spring.

2 As the lane emerges from the trees go through a small iron gate up on the left and along the bottom field edge to a ladder-stile. Go along the next field edge to another ladder-stile, then follow the boundary on your right. At its corner keep ahead across the large field – *enjoying views across to Anglesey* – to a gate at a wood corner onto the bend of a road. Turn RIGHT up the road – *with a good view east along the coast* – soon bending right – *with extensive views of Penrhyn Castle, Bangor and Anglesey.* Later, beyond Bronydd Isaf, you are joined by the North Wales Path. At the junction keep ahead. Shortly after passing the driveway to Llwyn Penddu Uchaf, turn RIGHT on the signposted North Wales Path along an access track to a kissing gate/gate and on past Plas Uchaf to a gate. Just beyond go down the track's left fork to gates, then down the enclosed green track to another gate. Follow the green track down a large field, soon bending past a wood to a gate. The walled track continues beside the wood.

WALK 3

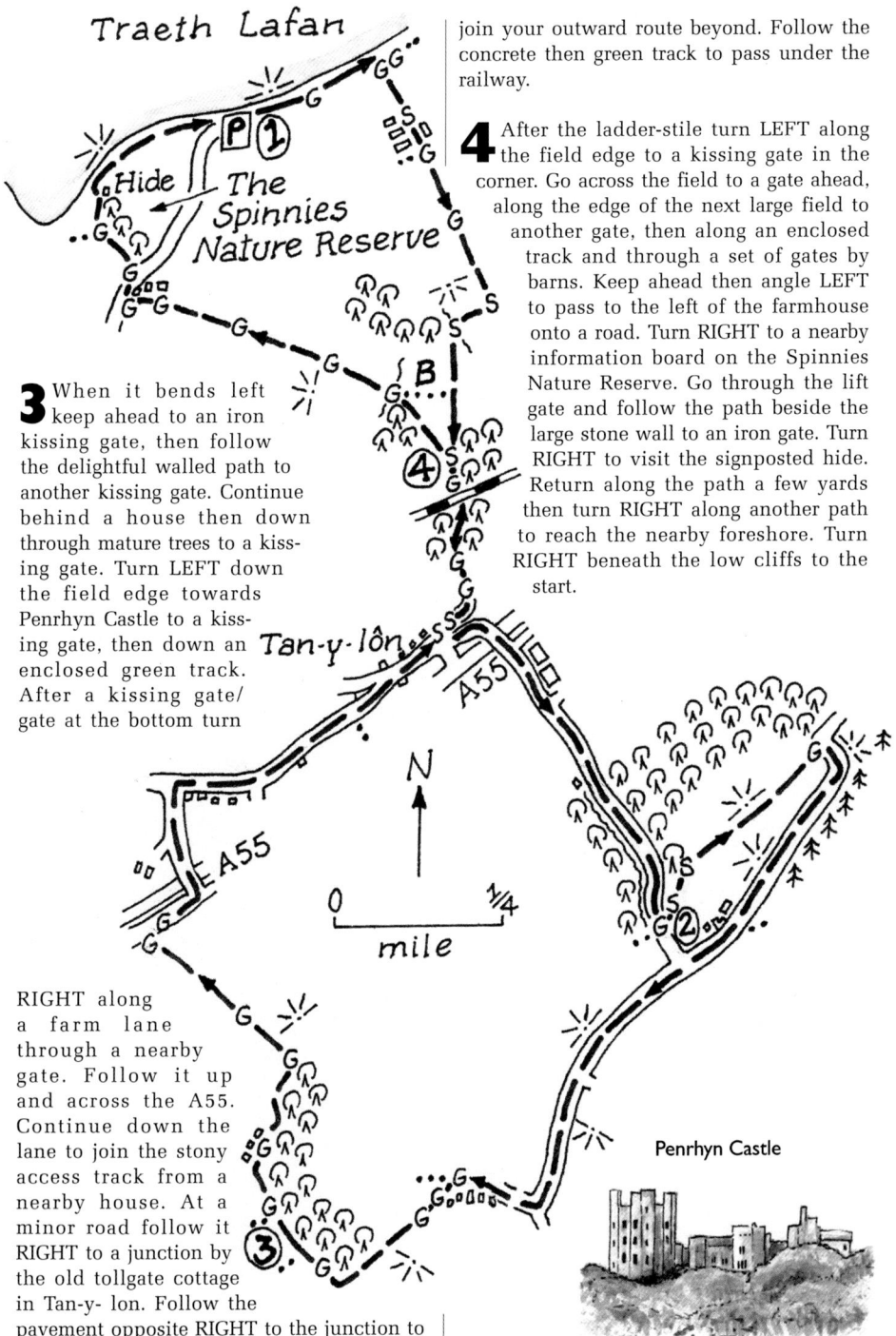

join your outward route beyond. Follow the concrete then green track to pass under the railway.

4 After the ladder-stile turn LEFT along the field edge to a kissing gate in the corner. Go across the field to a gate ahead, along the edge of the next large field to another gate, then along an enclosed track and through a set of gates by barns. Keep ahead then angle LEFT to pass to the left of the farmhouse onto a road. Turn RIGHT to a nearby information board on the Spinnies Nature Reserve. Go through the lift gate and follow the path beside the large stone wall to an iron gate. Turn RIGHT to visit the signposted hide. Return along the path a few yards then turn RIGHT along another path to reach the nearby foreshore. Turn RIGHT beneath the low cliffs to the start.

3 When it bends left keep ahead to an iron kissing gate, then follow the delightful walled path to another kissing gate. Continue behind a house then down through mature trees to a kissing gate. Turn LEFT down the field edge towards Penrhyn Castle to a kissing gate, then down an enclosed green track. After a kissing gate/gate at the bottom turn RIGHT along a farm lane through a nearby gate. Follow it up and across the A55. Continue down the lane to join the stony access track from a nearby house. At a minor road follow it RIGHT to a junction by the old tollgate cottage in Tan-y-lon. Follow the pavement opposite RIGHT to the junction to

WALK 4
CEGIN VALLEY

DESCRIPTION A 5 mile (**A**) walk exploring the attractive countryside adjoining Bangor. The route rises from the town centre to the hamlet of Minfordd, then crosses enclosed upland pasture, offering extensive mountain views. After quiet country roads it follows a section of the former Penrhyn quarry narrow gauge railway along the attractive narrow wooded Cegin valley- known as Lôn Bach and now part of the longer surfaced Lôn Las Ogwen recreational trail – to historic Porth Penrhyn, that it once served. Allow about 2½ hours. An alternative 2¾ mile walk (**B**) from the Clock Tower is included.

START Beach Road long stay car park, A5 Bangor [SH 587727] or Clock Tower, High Street [SH 583721].

DIRECTIONS The signposted shoreline car park adjoins the A5 near Kwik-fit on the eastern side of Bangor.

*B*y the end of the 18thC Penrhyn slate quarry at Bethesda had become a significant commercial undertaking that required a more efficient means of transport of slate to Port Penrhyn. In 1801 the Penrhyn estate built a 2ft narrow gauge railroad between the quarry and the port, incorporating at its northern end a section of the existing 1 mile Llandegai tramway used between 1798-1831 to transport flint & stone from a mill at Llandegai to the nearby port. The single line, with passing places, and inclines was 6 miles long and ran just to the west of the Afon Ogwen. Quarried slate was first taken to Felin Fawr mill at Coed-y-Parc for processing then conveyed by horse-drawn wagons to the port. The railroad significantly reduced transport costs and by the mid 19thC trains of up to 50 wagons were passing daily along the line. The building of the standard gauge LNWR branch line to Porth Penrhyn in 1852 from the Chester – Holyhead main line railway provided a link for the Penrhyn railway to the developing national railway network. In 1879 a new transport phase began with the opening of a new route for the narrow gauge railway via the Cegin valley, which avoided inclines and allowed steam locomotives to be used. The Penrhyn quarry railway operated until 1962, and a year later the LNWR branch line closed. Parts of both former railway lines have been incorporated into the Lôn Bach recreational trail.

1 Go through barriers and cross the road by the nearby Pelican Crossing to go along Ambrose Street opposite. Shortly bend LEFT along Friar's Road then at the junction turn RIGHT along High Street. At the next junction by the Spinnies/North Wales Wildlife Trust continue ahead along the no through road through the busy shopping area, soon pedestrianised.

2 At the Victorian clock tower continue along the High Street. At its pedestrianised end by the cathedral (worth a visit – see Walk 1 for information) turn LEFT. Follow the road past Varsity then the imposing Capel Pendref. About 50 yards further go up railed steps on the left and follow the signposted enclosed path rising steadily passing above a church and a railway tunnel. When the path splits by a seat continue up the left fork beside the wall. At a road continue along the pavement then when it bends left follow the minor road ahead signposted to Pentir/Caerhuner, soon passing through Minfordd. Continue along this quiet country road past the entrance to Bryn Glas.

3 Shortly, cross a ladder-stile on the left opposite an access lane. Go along the field edge to another ladder-stile then follow the left-hand edge of the next small field to a kissing gate. Keep ahead along a faint narrow green track – *enjoying great views to Ogwen valley and Tryfan*. After about 30 yards as it begins to descend by a slate boundary – with a view of Bangor University,with Great Orme and Penmaenmawr mountain beyond – angle LEFT along a grass shelf to a kissing gate. Keep ahead along the next large field – *enjoying extensive views* – to another kissing gate. Continue along the next field edge and down to a kissing gate onto a road. Follow it LEFT, then turn RIGHT down Lon Cefn. (For **Walk B** continue along the road, then follow

8

WALK 4

another as shown down to Bangor.) Follow the minor road down past a farm and under a former railway bridge of the LNWR Bethesda branch line (1884-1963).

4 After crossing a footbridge over the Afon Cegin by a ford, known locally as 'The White Bridge' go through a bridle gate on the right to join the Lon Bach recreational trail by an information board welcoming you to the Cegin valley. Turn LEFT on cycle route 5 under the road bridge, then go along the wide surfaced route of the 1879 built narrow gauge railway, soon passing under the tall arched mainline railway bridge. Continue through the delightful wooded valley near the river. The trail passes under the A5 – now *following the route shared by the narrow gauge railway and the adjoining Porth Penrhyn LNWR branch line – crosses the river twice and continues to pass under a stone Penrhyn Estate road bridge. Before it was built in 1820 small vessels could access a tidal pool and quay here to load with slate transported from Penrhyn Quarry. Just beyond you reach the access road to nearby Port Penrhyn. By the early 19thC it was a developing industrial site with a slate and flint mills.* Follow it LEFT up to join the Penrhyn Estate road to reach the A5. Turn RIGHT and follow the roadside cycle/walkway back to the start.

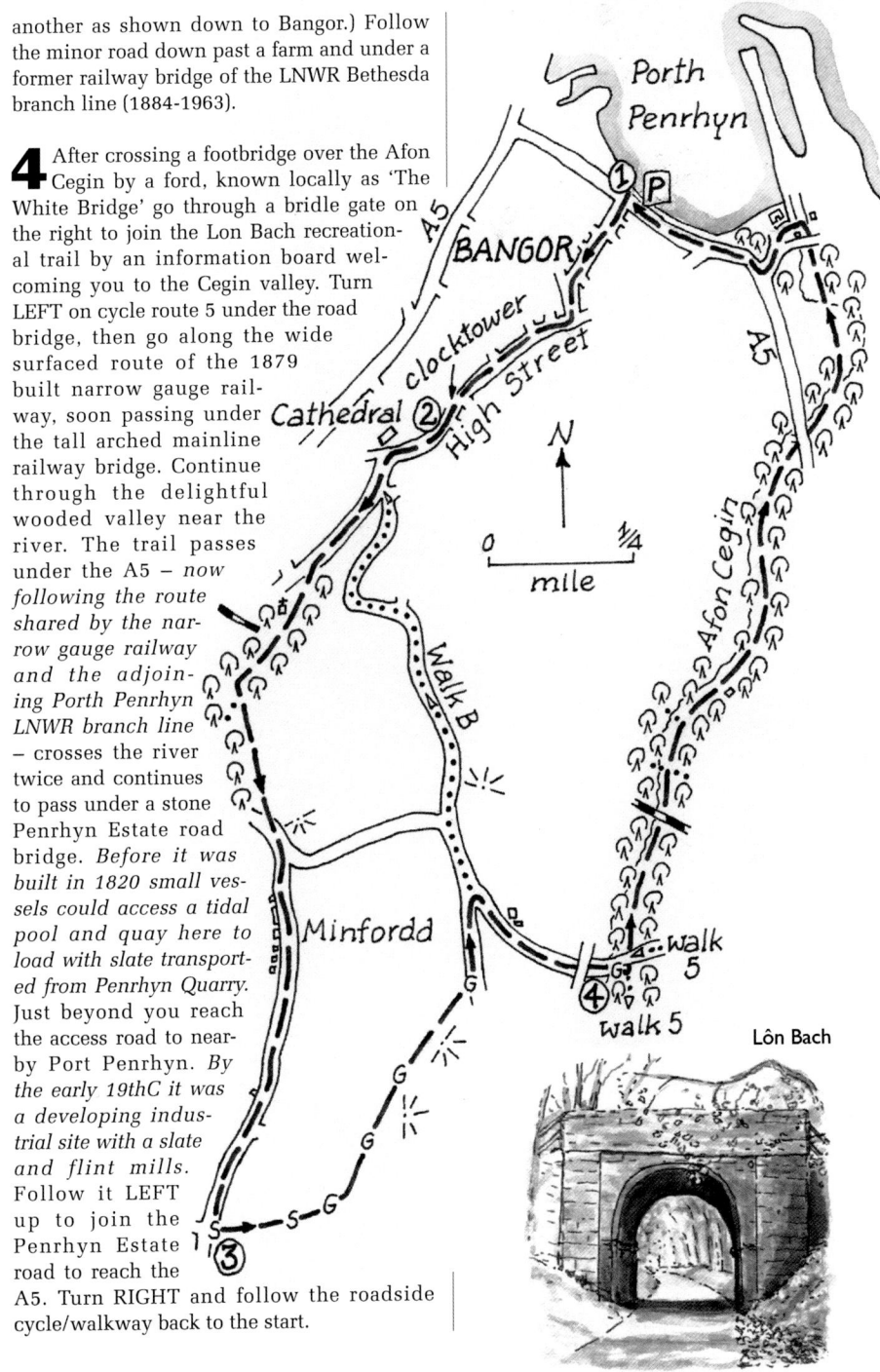

Lôn Bach

9

WALK 5
LON LAS OGWEN

DESCRIPTION A 6¼ mile walk exploring the countryside between Llandygai and Tregarth. After a short section of the North Wales Path, the route heads south along the Lôn Las Ogwen, a surfaced recreational trail for walkers, cyclists and horse riders. The first section of the trail, also known as Lôn Bach, follows the former Penrhyn Quarry narrow gauge railway (1879-1962) along the delightful wooded Cegin valley to Glasinfryn (see Walk 4 for more information on the railway's history), then a section of the former Bethesda branch railway line (1884-1963) to Tregarth, before returning north on mainly field paths via two crossings of the Afon Ogwen. Allow about 3½ hours.
START Road junction, Llandygai [SH 598706].
DIRECTIONS Follow the A5 south from Bangor. At a mini-roundabout turn left signposted to Llandegai/Tal-y-bont, past the nearby entrance to Penrhyn Castle. Take the first road on the right signposted to the rugby ground, to find roadside parking on the no through road beyond the next junction.

1 Return to the nearby junction and turn LEFT up the road's right-hand side, then turn RIGHT up the signposted Wales Coast Path to the nearby A5. Cross to a kissing gate opposite and follow the signposted enclosed North Wales Path past a railway tunnel ventilation shaft to a kissing gate onto a minor road. Follow it LEFT. After just over ½ mile it crosses a bridge into the Cegin valley. Just before the old footbridge and ford across the river go through a bridle gate to an information board on the valley to join the Lôn Las Ogwen. Follow the former narrow gauge railway south through the narrow wooded Cegin valley, later passing through a cutting high above the river. After almost 1 mile the recreational route leaves the valley and passes under the A55 at Glasinfryn. It then crosses a viaduct and continues along the former Bangor-Bethesda branch line – *built by London and North West Railways and which carried both goods and passengers. Later it crosses the A4244 by an impressive modern bridge*. After passing under two road bridges it heads east to reach the road at Tregarth. Follow it through the village past an imposing chapel. *Tregarth, which developed around slate, is perhaps best known for a street of houses built by Lord Penrhyn for workers who did not join in the great strike of 1900-03. It is known locally as 'Stryd y Gynffon' (Traitors Row).*

2 Just beyond the junction you rejoin Lôn Las Ogwen, on the left. After descending to the Community Centre it heads through a recreational area then continues through trees to pass under two bridges – *with a view of the original impressive railway cutting* – to join a minor road above. Turn LEFT down the road. At the junction go up the road ahead. On the bend, keep ahead up a minor road. Shortly take a signposted path along an access track on the right just before Tan-y-Cae road on the left. (After heavy rain the next section can be muddy. If so use the alternative path shown further along the road to point 3.) After a few yards go through an old iron gate on the left in trees and follow the path to a kissing gate, and on through trees. After another kissing gate the path continues through trees to a junction with the alternative path. Here turn RIGHT.

3 Emerging from trees follow the hedge on your right down to a kissing gate, then an enclosed path down to pass between dwellings. Go down the access track, then on the bend go through a kissing gate ahead, and down the path's right fork to a kissing gate onto a road. Turn LEFT to the nearby junction with the A5 and follow the pavement opposite across the nearby road bridge over the Afon Ogwen. At the house on the bend turn LEFT down its short access lane and on down to a kissing gate and a slab slate bridge over a stream. Follow the path beside the fence above the mature tree-lined river. At the fence corner angle RIGHT up the field to go through a waymarked gate. Go along the right-hand field edge, soon joining an access track. After a kissing gate/gate go through the nearby kissing gate, where you join the North Wales Path. Follow the slate boundary along the edge of three fields, through

WALK 5

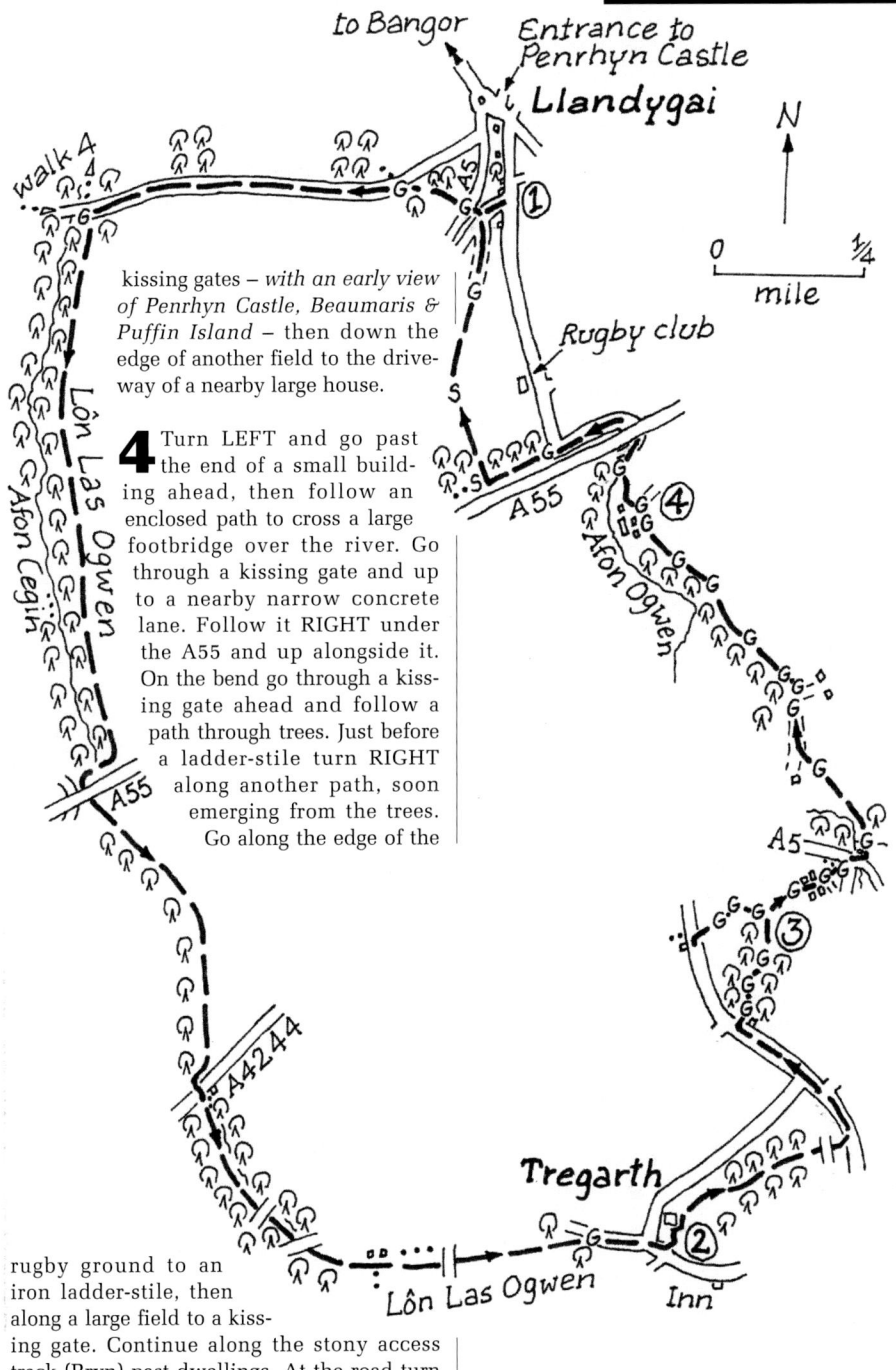

kissing gates – *with an early view of Penrhyn Castle, Beaumaris & Puffin Island* – then down the edge of another field to the driveway of a nearby large house.

4 Turn LEFT and go past the end of a small building ahead, then follow an enclosed path to cross a large footbridge over the river. Go through a kissing gate and up to a nearby narrow concrete lane. Follow it RIGHT under the A55 and up alongside it. On the bend go through a kissing gate ahead and follow a path through trees. Just before a ladder-stile turn RIGHT along another path, soon emerging from the trees. Go along the edge of the rugby ground to an iron ladder-stile, then along a large field to a kissing gate. Continue along the stony access track (Bryn) past dwellings. At the road turn RIGHT down to the start.

WALK 6
MOEL FABAN, LLEFN & GYRN

DESCRIPTION A 5½ mile walk (**A**), generally on good paths, exploring the attractive upland landscape near Bethesda, featuring three outlying foothills of the Carneddau range, offering extensive coastal and mountain views. The route rises from Bethesda into Open Access land, then climbs up and across Moel Faban (1342 ft/409 metres) before gently descending to a point overlooking the narrow pass of Bwlch ym Mhwll-le. From its eastern end the route makes a short climb onto the grassy top of nearby Llefn (1453 ft/443 metres), then continues up to the summit of Gyrn (1778 ft/542 metres). The walk returns through Bwlch ym Mhwll-le or via its northern rim (route b), then the lower western slope of Moel Faban. Allow about 3½ hours. Avoid in poor visibility. A less demanding but equally enjoyable 3 mile walk (**B**) omitting Llefn and Gyrn is included.
START Top car park, Bethesda [SH 624668].
DIRECTIONS In the centre of Bethesda take the road signposted to the Police station, library and car park. A road on the right leads to the car park.

1 From the north eastern corner of the car park join a stony access track. Follow it up past a small stone building, then take a path's right fork up through trees to a road. Turn RIGHT past the side road of Bryn Teg and continue along the road (Stryd Cefnfaes) to crossroads. Go to the no through road opposite (Ffordd Ffrydlas), then immediately turn LEFT up an initially stepped enclosed surfaced path to a road above. Turn RIGHT then LEFT up Cilfodan. Follow it up into open country to its end by Tanyfoel terraced cottages. Continue ahead on a signposted path up an initially walled access track, then when it bends towards a house continue ahead up a delightful part walled path to a kissing gate into Open Access land.

2 Go straight up the slope ahead, over a stream, and follow a clear path up the gorse covered southern slope of Moel Faban, then across its stone covered summit featuring two large stone shelters. *There are great views to Bangor, Penrhyn Castle, Menai Strait, Traeth Lafan and Anglesey beyond, and a panorama of mountains inland. Ahead is Llefn and the shapely peak of Gyrn.* The path now descends to a cross-path overlooking the narrow pass of Bwlch ym Mhwll-le. (For **Walk B** follow the improving path left down to join a wide path at point 4.) Follow it RIGHT down to cross a reedy area at the end of the bwlch. Now head up towards Llefn, soon crossing a wide cross-path.

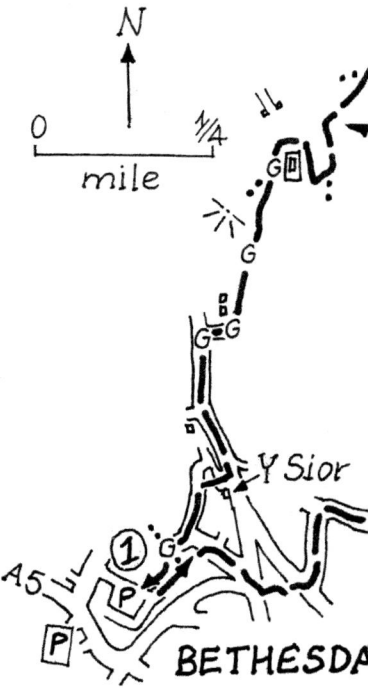

Continue across the gorse and stone covered ground, soon climbing more steeply to the left of scree to follow a good path across Llefn's grassy summit – *soon with a reservoir visible down to the left.* The path now heads towards Gyrn, goes over a cross-path, then begins to rise, soon more steeply, to briefly join a wider path. Head across the left shoulder of the nearby rocky summit, then turn RIGHT up onto the final top with its small stone shelter – *with new views into a wild upland landscape overlooked by Moel Wnion*

WALK 6

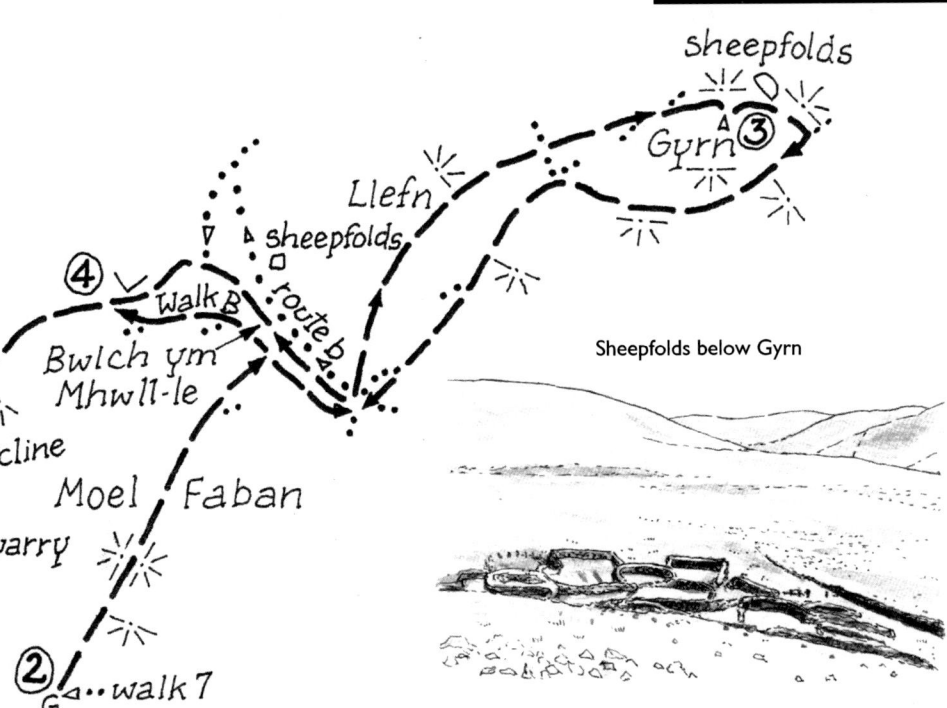

Sheepfolds below Gyrn

ahead and the nearby mountain tops of Drosgl, Bera Mawr & Bera Bach.

3 Descend north east to overlook a complex of sheepfolds, then work your way down the stone covered slope to their right hand end. Continue south east down the slope for about 50 yards, then turn RIGHT along a narrow cross-path. The improving path heads south-west then west down beneath Gyrn, passing a small quarry. At a crossroad of paths take the wide path half-LEFT (south-west) to pass beneath the eastern slopes of Llefn. Continue down the path's wider left fork and past another path angling right. At a cross-path keep ahead, bending RIGHT to the reedy area at the end of Bwlch ym Mhwll-le. (For the alternative **Route B** follow the cross-path right along the northern rim of the bwlch, then down beneath large sheepfolds to join a wide path at a wall corner. Follow it left down to the bottom of the bwlch and on to point 4.) Follow a path along the left hand side of the narrow pass, soon descending through it to join the bend of a wide path. Follow it LEFT to pass a fence corner.

4 Continue with the delightful wide path across the lower gorse covered western slopes of Moel Faban. After briefly joining a wall continue with the wide path (an old tramway) across the hillside, over an old incline, past a quarry and across an area of waste. As it begins to rise, angle RIGHT down past a large 'wall' of slate waste, then just before a boundary wall turn RIGHT down past the perimeter fence of a covered reservoir. Follow the fence round to a kissing gate. Follow the main path down through gorse and small trees, across quarry waste to another kissing gate, then down to a kissing gate/gate by a house. Go down its access lane to a road. Follow it LEFT past houses. At a junction by Y Sior pub, turn RIGHT past a slate sculpture at a viewing area, and down a stepped walled path to a road. Follow the pavement opposite LEFT down past a children's play area. At the bottom junction by terraced houses turn RIGHT down to go through a large kissing gate. Follow a stony path LEFT down through an open area of small trees to the car park.

WALK 7
FELIN FAWR

DESCRIPTION A 6 mile walk exploring the varied countryside around Bethesda, featuring historic Felin Fawr Works, rivers, waterfalls, woodland, enclosed upland pasture, a delightful section of the Lôn Las Ogwen recreational trail and good views. Allow about 3½ hours. The route can easily be shortened to a 4½ mile (**B**) or 3½ mile (**C**) walk.
START Top car park, Bethesda [SH 624668].
DIRECTIONS See Walk 6.

Felin Fawr Works developed from the beginning of the 19th C into the main mill and workshop site for Penrhyn Quarry. Slate from the quarry was first brought in wagons to the site for processing by a narrow gauge railway, initially horse-drawn then from 1879 pulled by small steam locomotives, before continuing to Porth Penrhyn. The site eventually contained two slab mills, a foundry, joiner's shop, manager's house and a locomotive shed. Waterwheels provided power for the complex until about 1930. The Penrhyn railway closed in 1962 and the Works in 1965. The historic buildings were restored in the 1990s and are now used as light industrial units.

1 From the south-western corner of the car park descend steps, go down a wide paved path between houses. When it splits keep ahead down steps and on to the High Street. Cross to the pavement opposite and follow it RIGHT through Bethesda. Just after Londis shop, turn LEFT along Station Road, past the nearby Medical Centre, then follow a wide surfaced riverside path to cross a footbridge over the Afon Ogwen. Go up the stony handrailed path ahead past woodland to a kissing gate and along an access track to the nearby road. Turn LEFT. On the bend go up the road on the right signposted to Lôn Las Ogwen/Felin Fawr Workshops. Take the signposted cycle/walkway round the left hand edge of the Felin Fawr site. Go past the large locomotive shed being used by Penrhyn Railway Heritage Trust for restoring a section of the narrow gauge railway, then pass under the road bridge. Go along the wide stony Lon Las Ogwen, soon bending LEFT and continuing beneath quarry spoil heaps, later passing high above the valley road, before bending south through trees. *(For information on the former quarry railway see Walk 4.)*

2 At the Penrhyn Quarry access road go through the gate opposite and continue along the recreational route above the river tumbling through an impressive gorge, then rising past a waterfall to reach Pont Ogwen. Cross the bridge over the river, then turn RIGHT up Ogwen Bank Caravan Park's access road to the A5. Take the signposted path opposite up through trees, over a forestry track, and up through mixed woodland to a small iron gate. At a nearby large forestry track turning area continue ahead following an old track up through the wood, soon becoming a path. Shortly the path begins a steady descent through trees to a small iron gate onto a narrow lane. (For **Walk C** turn left to a nearby junction and follow roads as shown to point 6.)

3 Turn RIGHT along the lane it to its end, then turn LEFT between houses and an outbuilding to an iron gate. The signposted path rises through the wood above the river, passing a delightful waterfall. Soon afterwards, the path, guided by yellow topped poles, moves away from the river through trees then a more open aspect to a kissing gate. Continue ahead past a post and across a field – *with imposing Carnedd Dafydd ahead* – through a wall gap, then angle slightly RIGHT to a gate, over a stream and on past another post Angle RIGHT up to join a track which you follow to the nearby farm. Follow its access road past a house and down to cross a bridge over the river. Turn LEFT down the road. At a junction turn RIGHT up Ciltwllan – *offering great views of the Carneddau mountains*. (For **Walk B** keep ahead and follow roads as shown to point 6.)

4 Just before the road ends at the final house cross an iron ladder-stile on the left and follow the signposted path (way-

WALK 7

marked 4 Valleys Walk) near the fence on your left up the reedy field to a ladder-stile. Work your way across the next field to cross an iron ladder-stile in the wall ahead. Follow the wall on your right to cross another iron ladder-stile. Angle LEFT up to join a green track by the wall and follow it past the nearby farm. Continue along its access lane then after a gated cattle grid turn RIGHT along the

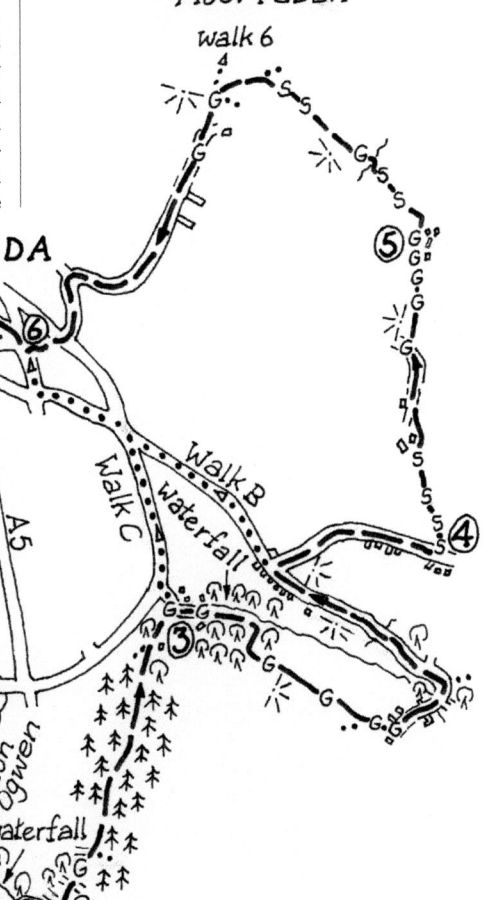

edge of two fields through kissing gates. Keep ahead to a small facing gate by a house.

5 Just beyond the house go through a waymarked gate on the left. Follow the wall on your right, then turn LEFT across an area of young trees to a ladder-stile. Go straight across the next field to a stile then angle LEFT to a nearby red topped post and bend RIGHT down to stepping stones over a stream to a small gate beyond. Follow a path angling up the slope just ahead to another post Go straight ahead across a large rough reedy field, over an old boundary wall, and on over sleeper bridges to a ladder-stile in the corner. Turn LEFT along the next field edge to an old iron ladder-stile into an Open Access area beneath Moel Faban grazed by wild ponies. Continue ahead, soon joining a wide green path to reach a kissing gate. Go down the delightful part walled path, then a nearby house's access track, soon walled, to join a minor road by Tanyfoel terraced cottages. Follow the road down to a junction at the edge of Bethesda. Turn RIGHT then take a surfaced enclosed path on the left down to another road. Turn RIGHT.

6 At the crossroads go along Stryd Cefnfaes opposite. At its end angle LEFT down to a large kissing gate. Turn LEFT and follow a stony path down through an open area of small trees to the car park.

WALK 8
COED-Y-PARC

DESCRIPTION A 3 mile walk exploring the undulating countryside immediately west of Bethesda. The route passes through attractive woodland and the small communities of Coed-y-Parc and Bryn Eglwys, before returning via woodland and a riverside path. Allow about 2 hours.
START Riverside car park, Bethesda [SH 622667].
DIRECTIONS The car park is signposted from the High Street in Bethesda, and accessed via Cae Star.

1 Follow the car park's exit road then turn RIGHT along the High Street. Take the first narrow road on the right to cross a footbridge over the Afon Ogwen. Follow the main surfaced path ahead past a play area, then an old tennis court among woodland. After gates follow a narrow tarmaced lane through open woodland to a road. Follow it RIGHT, then at the next junction at Coed-y-Parc, turn LEFT signposted to Mynydd Llandygai to cross a bridge over the former Penrhyn quarry railway line at the historic Felin Fawr Works site (see Walk 7 for information).

2 Here turn RIGHT along Tai'r Stablau past a waterfall in the trees. On the bend turn LEFT to a nearby kissing gate. Go up the enclosed path, soon bending RIGHT at a path junction up to another kissing gate. Go past cottages then turn LEFT up the road, soon passing the church at Bryn Eglwys. On the bend take the signposted path on the right past the end of 'The Milton' to a kissing gate and on up open tree-covered ground to a seat at a good viewpoint. Continue with the path through trees, shortly descending past two side paths to a kissing gate. Follow the enclosed path to another kissing gate, then go along a field edge to a kissing gate at a road end.

3 Here, turn RIGHT past gorse then descend the field to a kissing gate on your right. Follow the clear path down to another kissing gate, soon afterwards descending through attractive woodland. When it splits go down the left fork, over a cross-path to a small gate below to pass under the former railway line and on to reach Tanysgafell road. Turn RIGHT then LEFT along a nearby access track to cottages, then follow an enclosed path to a kissing gate and on to cross a footbridge over the Afon Ogwen. Follow the riverside path then road to the main street in Bethesda. Follow it RIGHT back to the start.

WALK 9
MYNYDD LLANDEGAI

DESCRIPTION A 5 mile walk (A) of great variety. The route heads west to Coed-y-Parc, skirts the huge spoil tips of Penrhyn Quarry, then follows quarrymen's paths across the edge of an expansive treeless area to Mynydd Llandegai, a village built for Penrhyn quarry workers in the 19thC. It then returns via the attractive woodland of Parc yr Ocar and a section of riverside walking. Allow about 3 hours. A shorter 2¾ mile walk (B) is included.
START As Walk 8.

1 Follow instructions in paragraph 1 of Walk 8.

2 Continue up the road past reservoirs built in the 1840s to provide water to drive waterwheels at Felin Fawr Works. Just before the entrance to Yr Ocar take a signposted path through a gate on the left. (For **Walk B** go down Yr Ocar's access track, then cross a nearby footbridge over the river to a join the main route in Parc Yr Ocar.) Go along the edge of two fields, then angle LEFT down the next to a ladder-stile in the corner. Go to a kissing gate ahead, then along an access track past Weirglodd. On the bend follow the signposted path ahead beneath vast quarry spoil tips to a ladder-stile. (The next section is guided by red marks on trees and stones.) Keep ahead, soon joining a good path a little way from the tips. When you rejoin the tips the path bends RIGHT up to an old ruin. Angle slightly LEFT up the rough pasture

WALK 8 & 9

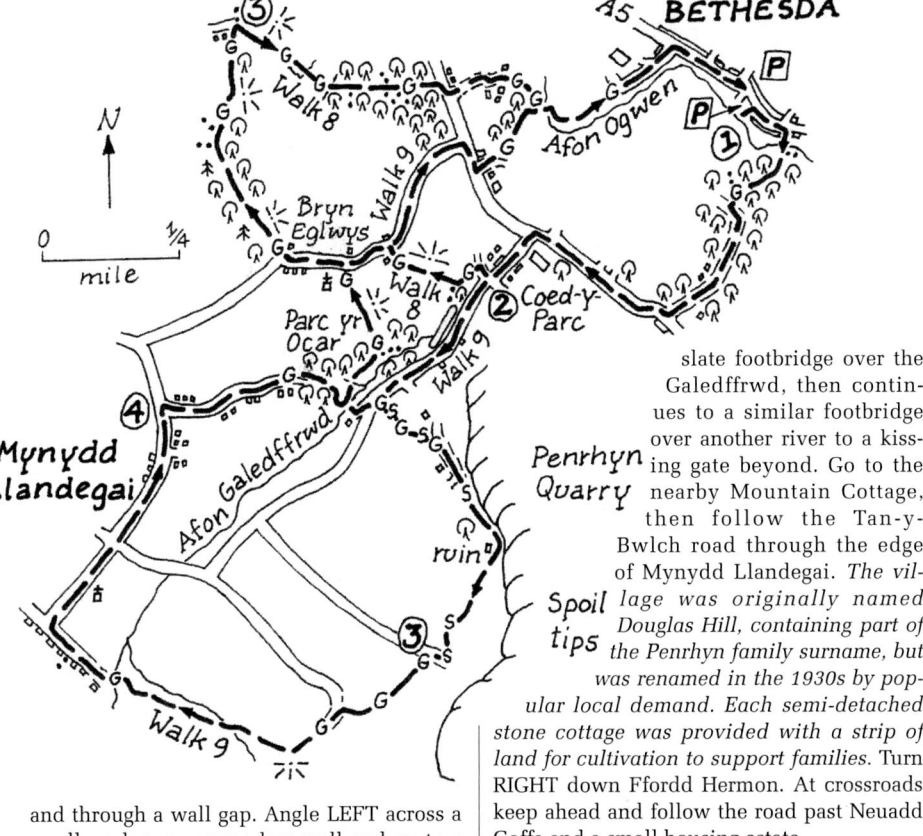

and through a wall gap. Angle LEFT across a small enclosure, over a low wall and on to a ladder-stile. Go across the reedy pasture to a ladder-stile in the top left-hand corner onto a road end. Turn RIGHT.

3 Soon go through a kissing gate on the left and head up the field to another kissing gate into Open Access land. Head towards telegraph poles, then after 20 yards follow a path RIGHT to a farm track. Follow it LEFT to a gate. Follow the good path beside the wall – *enjoying a good view of the huge Penrhyn Quarry* – at the end of the 19thC, employing 3,000 men, the largest slate quarry in the world. Unfortunately Lord Penrhyn's wealth alienated the poorly paid quarrymen, resulting in long and volatile strikes. At its corner the well made quarrymen's path angles RIGHT along the edge of an expansive area of tussocky open ground – *a Site of Special Scientific Interest* – crosses a slab slate footbridge over the Galedffrwd, then continues to a similar footbridge over another river to a kissing gate beyond. Go to the nearby Mountain Cottage, then follow the Tan-y-Bwlch road through the edge of Mynydd Llandegai. *The village was originally named Douglas Hill, containing part of the Penrhyn family surname, but was renamed in the 1930s by popular local demand. Each semi-detached stone cottage was provided with a strip of land for cultivation to support families.* Turn RIGHT down Ffordd Hermon. At crossroads keep ahead and follow the road past Neuadd Goffa and a small housing estate.

4 Shortly afterwards turn RIGHT down a narrow no through road. When it becomes a track at Ynys Isaf go through a kissing gate into Parc Yr Ocar. Follow the wide path, initially beside the wall, down into the wooded valley. At a footbridge over the river, where you are joined by Walk B, continue with the woodland path, soon contouring high above the river, then take its left fork to a kissing gate. Go up the edge of two fields and on to join the road by the church in Bryn Eglwys. Turn RIGHT down the road. At the junction turn RIGHT, then LEFT briefly along Galedffrdd Mill's access track to a kissing gate ahead. Follow the path down to cross a footbridge over the Afon Ogwen. Follow the riverside path then road to the main street in Bethesda. Follow it RIGHT back to the start.

WALK 10
MOEL Y CI

DESCRIPTION A 5¼ mile (**A**) or 4½ mile (**B**) walk exploring the varied countryside south east of Tregarth, featuring extensive views. The route follows good paths to the hamlet of Sling, then rises through Y Parc, an Open Access area, and continues to nearby Parc y Bwlch forest Walk B heads west through Parc y Bwlch. Walk A continues to the edge of Mynydd Llandegai before following a good path up across the small heather covered hill of Moel y Ci (1299 feet/396 metres) and down its steeper north western slope to be joined by Walk B. The route returns across enclosed farmland to finish on a short section of the Lôn Las Ogwen recreational trail. Allow about 3½ hours for the main walk.
START Pant yr Ardd pub, Tregarth [SH 604679].
DIRECTIONS Follow A5 south towards Bethesda, then side road to Tregarth. There is roadside parking before or after the Pant yr Ardd.

Tregarth, which developed around slate, is perhaps best known for a street of houses built by Lord Penrhyn for workers who did not join in the great strike of 1900-03. It is known locally as 'Stryd y Gynffon' (Traitors Row).

1 Just to the east of the Pant yr Ardd take a signposted path up a driveway past cottages and on to a kissing gate. Follow the track ahead past more cottages, then at a track junction turn LEFT. Take the adjoining path up steps, then follow a wide path LEFT round beneath woodland to a kissing gate/gate, and past a path on the left to another kissing gate/gate. Continue along a delightful enclosed path through two small iron gates. After a kissing gate turn RIGHT down a path beside the wall. *Ahead lies the conifer covered top of Moel y Ci.* After a kissing gate continue through trees, then at a path junction turn LEFT across a footbridge over a stream. At a yellow topped post beyond an old boundary, ignore the good path continuing ahead, but angle RIGHT through an area of small trees. At a stony cross-path follow it RIGHT to a kissing gate onto a road at Sling. Turn LEFT then RIGHT up a narrow no through road.

2 Go through a kissing gate on the left into an Open Access area and follow a path up the bracken/gorse covered hillside of Y Parc. When it splits keep with the main left fork. At a cross-path just below the rocky gorse covered top follow it LEFT a few yards towards a walled enclosed house, before continuing up to the left of high ground, following a line of telegraph poles – *with good views looking back*. Go past the nearby wall with a kissing gate in it and follow it up to a kissing gate in the wall corner. Follow a path angling LEFT up across the gorse covered hillside parallel with the nearby Parc y Bwlch forest – *enjoying panoramic mountain views*. At a cross-path on a line of telegraph poles follow it RIGHT to a kissing gate into the forest to a track beyond. (For **Walk B** follow it right, then when it bends sharp right, go through a kissing gate ahead. Follow the path down and along the edge of two fields, then through an area of young trees. The path crosses a track, descends through the forest to a kissing gate, then beside its boundary wall, before continuing to join Walk A at point 4.)

3 Follow the track LEFT along the forest edge – *enjoying views of mountains and the vast Penrhyn Quarry* – soon joined by another forestry track. Continue along the minor road to crossroads in Mynydd Llandegai. Turn RIGHT. Soon after passing Tan-y-Bwlch take a signposted path through a kissing gate into Open Access land. Follow the good path across the gorse/heather covered lower slopes of Moel-y-Ci, soon rising steadily. At a kissing gate in the wall at a good viewpoint, go through the adjoining wide gap and follow the path angling up the slope, later rising more steeply to reach the wide heather top of Moel-y-Ci. Follow the path to cross its rocky top and on to a trig point and stone shelter at its northern end – *offering extensive views along the coast from The Rivals to the Great Orme, and across*

WALK 10

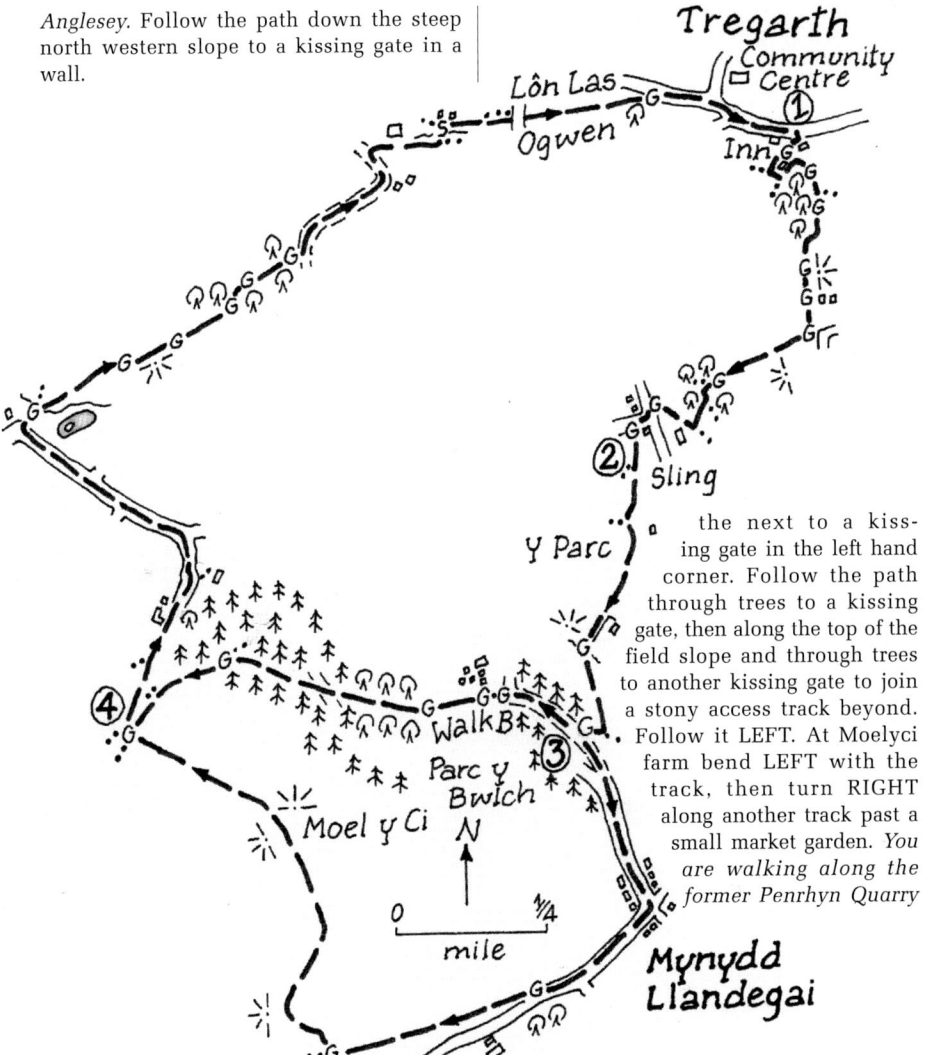

Anglesey. Follow the path down the steep north western slope to a kissing gate in a wall. the next to a kissing gate in the left hand corner. Follow the path through trees to a kissing gate, then along the top of the field slope and through trees to another kissing gate to join a stony access track beyond. Follow it LEFT. At Moelyci farm bend LEFT with the track, then turn RIGHT along another track past a small market garden. *You are walking along the former Penrhyn Quarry narrow gauge railway which carried wagons full of slate to Porth Penrhyn. (See Walk 4 for more information.) It is also part of an interesting heritage trail – leaflet available.* Soon, cross a footbridge over the stream to join the adjoining wide surfaced Lôn Las Ogwen trail – *on a section of the former Bangor–Bethesda LNWR railway line (1884-1963).* Follow it RIGHT, passing under a bridge, to eventually reach the road at Tregarth, which you follow back to the start.

4 Go through the kissing gate and turn RIGHT along a path down between walls to join a lane by Allt Uchaf. Follow it down to a junction and turn LEFT along the road, later passing a lake. On the bend by the Vicarage turn RIGHT along a signposted tree-lined path to a kissing gate by a stream. Go up the right hand edge of the large field, through a gateway in its corner and a kissing gate just beyond. Follow the path across the field to another kissing gate and on across

WALK 11
PARC DRYSGOL

DESCRIPTION A short but exhilarating undulating 3 mile walk, mainly on good paths, around a low upland area of Open Access land, reaching a height of 1247 ft/380 metres, and featuring changing mountain and coastal views. Allow about 2 hours.
START Road north east of Deiniolen [SH 584637].
DIRECTIONS On the northern side of Deiniolen go up a road signed to March Lyn. After nearly ¾ mile you will find a grass parking area on the left by a finger post (Rhiwlas 2 mile).

1 Go through the nearby kissing gate and follow the path up to a driveway. Go past the house, up steps to a small gate. Follow the delightful walled path up the hillside, then field edge to a small gate hidden in the wall ahead. Go up the next field edge to a kissing gate into Open Access land. Follow the path ahead across the heather covered terrain – *soon with a view of Moel y Ci, then Anglesey. To your left is Moel Rhiwen, which was once a deer park.* The path then steadily descends to a kissing gate by a small ruin. Pass between walls and mature trees, then angle LEFT away from the wall to follow a path down the hillside towards Rhiwlas.

2 At a waymark post, turn RIGHT and follow the wall on your left through two old boundaries, and down past trees, then go through a wall gap ahead. Angle RIGHT away from the wall and work your way across gorse covered terrain, past a waymarker post, and on up across more tussocky ground to a ladder-stile in the top boundary corner into Open Access land. Turn LEFT to follow a path beside the wall and through a gap in a facing wall. Ignore the ladder-stile, but follow a path angling RIGHT away from the wall, then continuing parallel with. Shortly take a slightly higher path passing a ladder-stile in the wall below.

3 A few yards from large stone gatepost in the wall ahead, turn RIGHT up a clear path (not one heading sharp right), passing close to a waymarker post After passing through an old gateway in a wall continue up the slope ahead – *soon with a good view of Penrhyn quarry with the Carneddau mountains beyond.* Just before a ladder-stile ahead, turn RIGHT and follow a fading path near the fence. A good path then parallels a wall, a few yards from it, up across the tussocky hillside to a wall corner on the shoulder of Parc Drysgol. Cross the wall on your left with care then follow a good path down beside the wall to the road. Follow it RIGHT past a forest. On the bend take a signposted path through a large iron gate and on to a gap in a wall corner. Follow a delightful wide walled path to a cottage and descend its access track to a road. Turn RIGHT along the grass verge to the start.

WALK 11 & 12

WALK 12
COED Y CLEGYR

DESCRIPTION A 3⅓ mile walk (**A**) around an attractive low upland part tree covered rocky area adjoining Padarn Country Park, featuring delightful walled paths and panoramic views to Llyn Padarn and Snowdon. Refreshments at 'The Caban' in Brynrefail centre makes a good finish to the walk. Allow about 2½ hours. An alternative 2 mile walk (**B**) is included.
START Brynrefail [SH 560629].
DIRECTIONS Brynrefail lies just off the A4244 near the junction with the A4086 by Llyn Padarn. There is roadside parking by a play area at the northern end of the village.

1 From the play area go along the road, over the river and past an access track (your return route). Take the first road on the left, soon rising and becoming a walled track which you follow to a cottage. Continue up the delightful narrow walled green track to its end at a ruined house. A path now rises to a red topped post, then bends LEFT and passes above another old dwelling to a slate stile onto a cross-path. (For **Walk B** follow it left to a kissing gate, then on, soon walled, past another walled path on the right. It soon bends to an old gateway, then continues to a farm's rough access track. Follow it to the minor road and the returning route.)

2 Turn RIGHT to pass above the ruined dwelling and between outbuildings into an open aspect. Continue along an intermittent walled section of path, soon rising past a side path to a kissing gate into Coed y Clegyr. Go past the Padarn Country Park sign and follow the path through trees, soon descending to a kissing gate then to a minor road. Go up the road, then follow it past various dwellings and viewpoints to Llyn Padarn and Snowdon. Later the road begins to rise steadily again – *with Dinorwic slate quarry ahead.*

3 Take a path on the left signposted to Deiniolen, opposite a no through road. Follow it up past a small quarry to a road at Maes Eilian. Follow it LEFT, then go along a narrow no through road on the left – *with a good view across to Deiniolen.* Shortly go down its right fork to its end by a house. Go through a small gate and down an enclosed path. At a kissing gate turn LEFT down the path between trees and on to join an access track by houses. At the bend of a nearby road follow its left fork through Clwt-y-bont. Later, after passing a side road over the river, then side tracks, the narrow road becomes rougher. At its end by a ruin go through a kissing gate on the waymarked Slate Trails path. Follow the undulating meandering path, sometimes walled, to a kissing gate and on to a farm. Follow its access track to the road at Brynrefail.

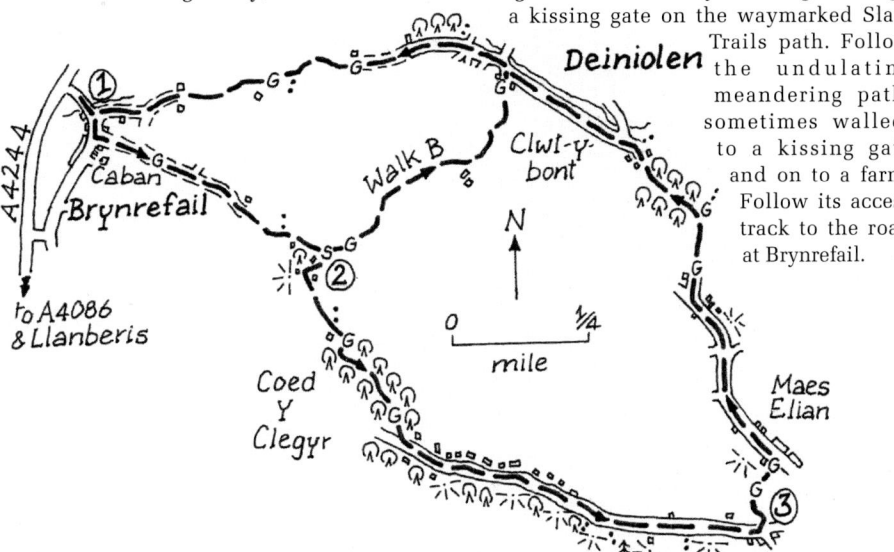

WALK 13
CEFN DDU

DESCRIPTION A 6 mile walk offering panoramic views to the top of Cefn Ddu (1446 ft/ 441 metres), from whose western slopes were transmitted the first ever morse code wireless message to Australia in 1918. The route follows a waymarked local community trail up to an upland road, then continues across the heather covered lower slopes of Cefn Ddu before following a fence up to a trig point on its summit. It then descends east and continues down through an old slate quarry and across upland pasture, before heading west along a scenic upland road to rejoin the community trail for a final descent to Waunfawr. Allow about 4½ hours. Avoid in poor visibility. The route can easily be divided as two separate walks: a lower level 2 mile walk following the community trail, or a 4 mile walk to Cefn Ddu starting from the car park beneath the quarry at the end of the minor upland road [SH 551599].
START War Memorial, Waunfawr [SH 525593].
DIRECTIONS Heading south east through the village you will find the War Memorial just past the second road on the left which leads to the school.

Waunfawr had a station on the North Wales Narrow Gauge Railway which opened in 1877 to carry dresed slate to Dinas Junction and in 2000 the station was reopened as part of the Welsh Highland Railway reconstruction.

1 Take the signposted enclosed path adjoining the Memorial to a kissing gate. After another kissing gate go up the left hand side of a field to two small iron gates at a crossroad of paths. Follow the enclosed one ahead to a kissing gate by a stream and one beyond to a road. Follow it RIGHT then turn LEFT up a signposted enclosed path past a cottage to another road. Turn RIGHT past other cottages, then on the bend follow a signposted enclosed path from a small gate up to another. The path now rises steadily beside a wall to a kissing gate. It then continues up the edge of two fields to another kissing gate and on up the next field to a small gate in the top corner. Turn RIGHT through a nearby wall gap and continue up beside the wall to a gate by a cottage. Go up its driveway then turn RIGHT up the road past two cottages and your return route.

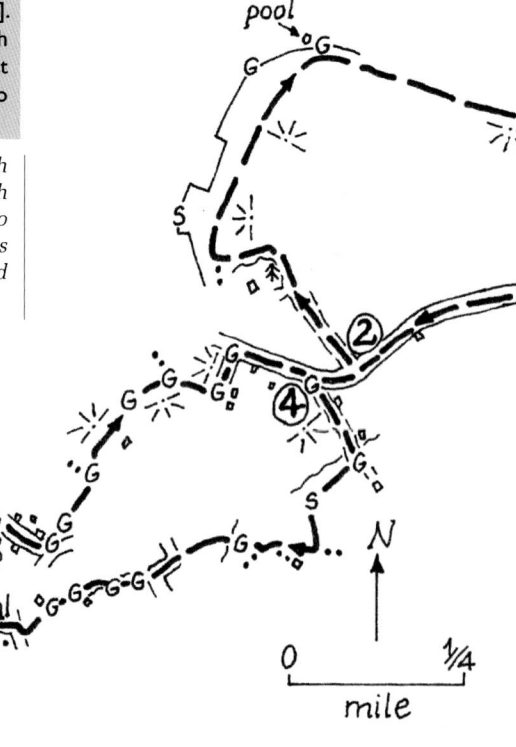

WALK 13

2 Just after the road bends go along a stony track signposted to Pendas Eithin across Open Access land. When the track ends at the entrance to the cottage keep ahead alongside the wall. At its corner turn LEFT down a path a few yards from it – *enjoying extensive views*. Go past another wall corner to join a distinctive cross-path 10 yards above a facing wall. Follow it RIGHT across the heather covered slope. When it peters out bend up to continue north along a nearby higher path. Eventually the path angles RIGHT towards a gate in the boundary ahead. *On the other side of the boundary, from 1914-39 and extending up the slope of Cefn Du, were ten 400 ft steel masts that held a vast aerial system linked to a Marconi wireless transmitting station located further downhill. Its purpose was to send messages to the USA but it is best known for its historic message in 1918. The aerial was dismantled in 1939.* Just before the gate turn RIGHT and follow the fence on a steady climb up the hillside to a trig point on Cefn Du's summit – *offering panoramic all round coastal and mountain views*. Just away down to pass between two small quarry buildings. A few yards beyond the path bends RIGHT down into the quarry, through a gap in the slate and down a small incline. After passing an old building, the path bends half-RIGHT – *now with a good view of Llyn Padarn and Llanberis* – to a small gate in a wall. Continue down a faint green track, past a waymark post, and follow a path to the wall corner ahead, then continue beside the wall. At its end and just before a building turn RIGHT along a green track to a gate and on to join another rough stony track. Follow it past a forest and a parking area. Continue west along the narrow scenic upland road beneath quarry tips later steadily descending to join your outward route at point 2. Continue down the road.

4 Take a signposted path (Hafod Oleu trail) through a kissing gate and follow the access track past Caer Gorlan and Grasbil to cross a sleeper bridge over a stream and go through a gate beyond. Turn RIGHT down a green track above the stream to a stile/gate. Continue down the delightful track towards the valley, soon bending RIGHT past a waymark post above a cottage, then joined by its green access track, At another waymark post angle RIGHT off the track to a small iron gate and a slab slate footbridge over a stream. Follow the waymarked path along the field edge, through a wall gap and down beside a wall. Go down an access lane and on its bend keep ahead to a kissing gate. Go down the field edge beside the stream to another kissing gate. Just beyond turn RIGHT across the stream then continue beside it to a kissing gate. Go down the field edge to a kissing gate by a house and down an enclosed path to a narrow road. Turn RIGHT and at the junction turn LEFT to a road by Cartrefle. Turn RIGHT to the nearby junction then LEFT along the road. At the junction turn RIGHT to join the main road in Waunfawr.

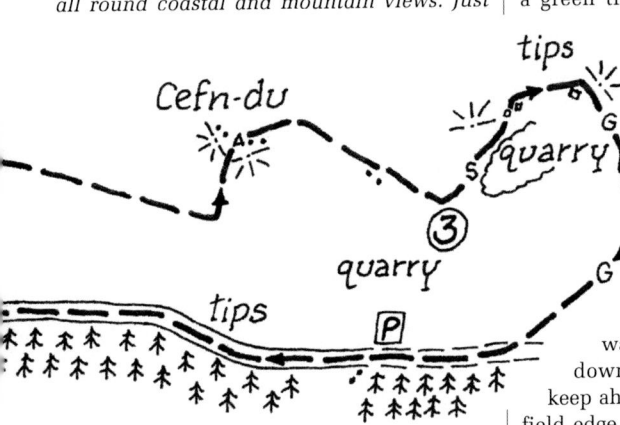

to the north is a large ruin, once part of the transmitting station system. Follow a path straight ahead down towards the distant vast Dinorwic quarry to join a fence/wall which you follow down to its corner.

3 Turn LEFT alongside the wall to a slate ladder-stile/gate. Now follow a path along the edge of a vast deep quarry, soon bending

23

WALK 14
PORT DINORWIC

DESCRIPTION An interesting 5 mile linear walk from Caernarfon to Y Felinheli, previously known as Port Dinorwic, a former slate port and now a popular marina, returning by frequent Arriva bus service 5/X5 (Bangor-Caernarfon). The route follows the first section of my Caernarfon town trail past the 13thC castle and Slate Quay, along the promenade, and through the Victoria Dock complex featuring a marina, waterside cafes and apartments. It then continues along the Lon Las Menai surfaced recreational trail, a section of the Wales Coast Path, largely following the former Bangor-Caernarfon railway line alongside the Menai Strait to Y Felinheli. Allow about 3 hours. The route can easily be started from Victoria Dock car park.
START Castle Square, Caernarfon [SH 479626] or Victoria Dock car park [SH 481633] (accessed from the A487 roundabout by Morrison's).

*P*ort Dinorwic, with its inner and outer docks, was built on the edge of the Menai Strait in the late 18thC to serve a new and expanding Dinorwic slate quarry near Llanberis. Slate was first taken by horse and cart, then from 1824 by a horse drawn narrow gauge (2ft) railway. Increased slate production required an improvement in the transport infrastructure, and the line was replaced by an unusual 4ft gauge railway, known as the Padarn Railway. At its peak in the 1860s over 700 small vessels worked the port each year carrying up to 80000 tons of slate. Despite increased competition from railways trade continued well into the 20thC, with Ireland and the Channel Islands being the main market after World War I. Nowadays the port is used for pleasure boating and sailing.

1-2 Follow instructions in paragraphs 1 & 2 of Walk 15 to the Victoria Dock complex.

3 Continue along the promenade past a short pier giving good views along the Menai Strait, then round to join the Lôn Las Menai, a recreational route for walkers and cyclists. The wide surfaced route follows the edge of the Menai Strait above the shore. Shortly take a narrow path nearer the shore past a stone circle and seats, soon rejoining Lôn Las Menai. After crossing a road continue with the tree-lined route, passing under two bridges and crossing another road by a trading estate entrance. After joining the A487 by a roundabout, Lôn Las Menai continues alongside the road signposted to Y Felinheli (past bus stops giving you an option for an early return), later tree-lined. It

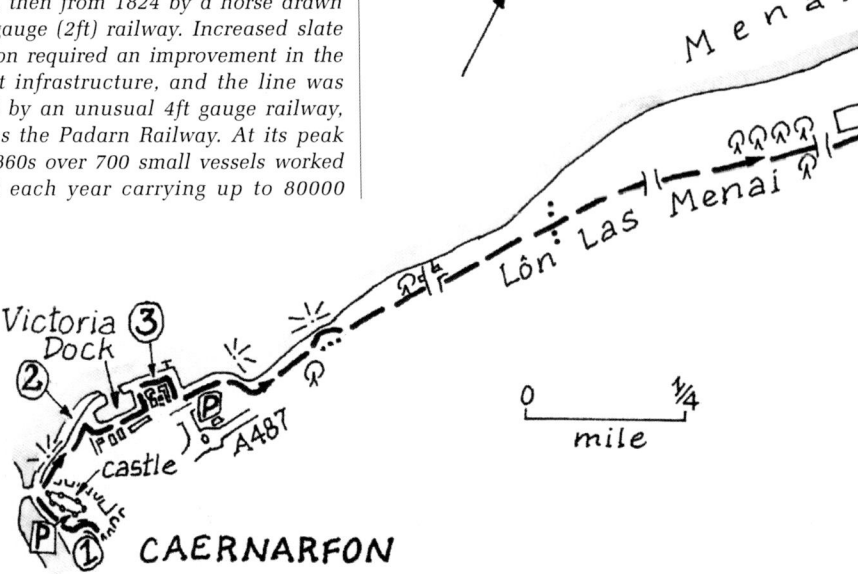

WALK 14

then angles away from the road to rejoin the former railway. After passing under a bridge the route continues through mature trees to reach a road at the outskirts of Y Felinheli. Go down the road and past boat workshops near the edge of the Menai Strait. After passing a small sailing centre go round the edge of a play area, then follow a surfaced path above the shore past seats to rejoin the road by toilets and the Garddfan Inn.

4 Immediately after the road bends right follow the stony signposted path and cycle route between houses, then go along a road through a housing estate. Shortly, divert along a short road on the left past a barrier, then a bricked path on the left for a view of the old dock, now a marina. Return to continue along the road. Soon, on your left, beyond a car park is a lock at the end of Port Dinorwic, controlled by a Dock Master, allowing access to and from the Menai Strait at high tide. A little further along the road cross a lift bridge over the Dinorwic marina, then do a circuit of its narrow upper section. Afterwards you may be tempted by refreshments in Yr Hen Lechan, before going up a railed stepped path at the end of hairdressers to the main road in Y Felinheli. Turn LEFT then cross to a bus stop on the opposite side for the return journey to Caernarfon.

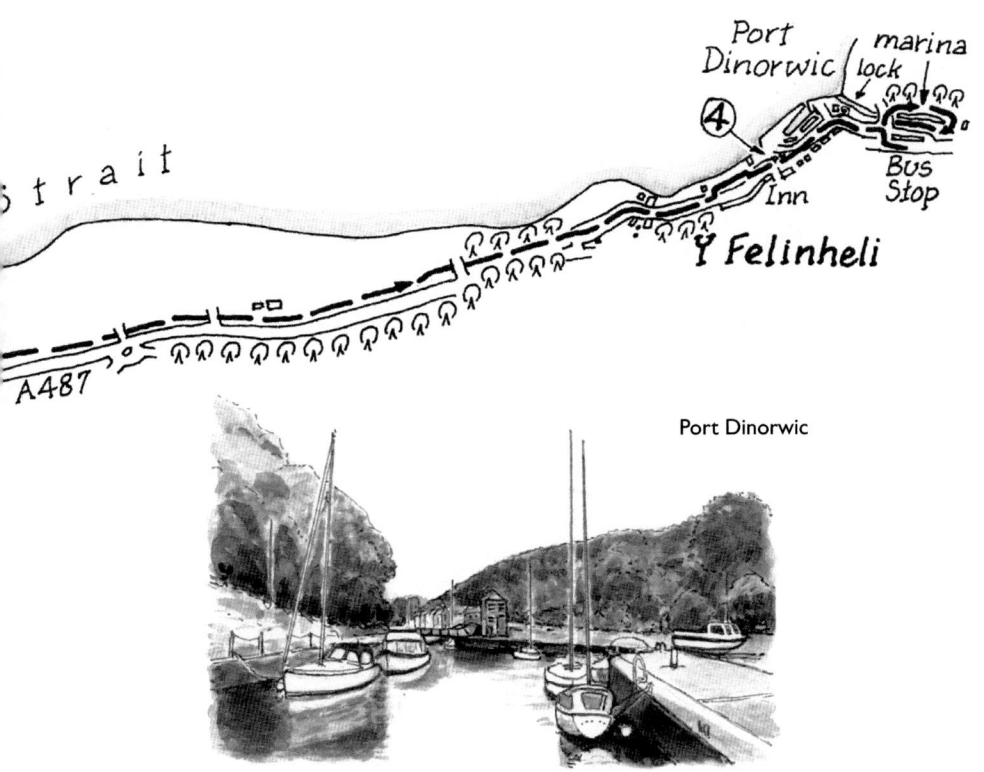

Port Dinorwic

WALK 15
CAERNARFON

DESCRIPTION An informative 2 mile walk exploring the historic old fortified walled town of Caernarfon, and Victoria Dock, featuring many places of interest It combines well with a visit to the impressive castle. Allow about 2 hours.
START Castle Square, Caernarfon [SH 479626].

*C*aernarfon *stands at the mouth of the river Seiont at the western end of The Menai Strait, with easy access to the sea and to nearby Anglesey. Its strategic location was key to its development. First the Romans established a fort here, named Segontium, about 80 AD and occupied it for over 300 years. It marked the western frontier of the Roman Empire. In the late 11thC the Normans built a motte and bailey castle here, which was then used as one of the courts of the Welsh Princes of Gwynedd.*

*T*he town *as we see it today was founded in the late 13thC after Edward I's conquest of Wales. In order to consolidate his control over the traditional Welsh Princes' heartland of North Wales he commissioned the building of a chain of coastal castles. Caernarfon castle, built on the site of the earlier motte and bailey fortification, is one of the most impressive. Work started on the castle and town walls in 1283, but was not completed until 1322. The walls, with eight towers and two gatehouses, encircled a new town laid out in a regular grid pattern of streets, and were designed to protect its English inhabitants. The castle became a seat of government and a Royal palace.*

*T*he 'bailey' *or small hill of the 11thC castle became part of Castle Green, now Castle Square (Y Maes). Since the late 13thC it has hosted weekly markets and at one time bull-baiting and cockfighting. The hill was taken down and its soil used to create Slate Quay in 1817. Caernarfon then became a bustling port exporting roofing slate, transported by rail from inland quarries.*

1 From the statue of Sir Hugh Owen, a leading educationalist, head towards the Castle, past an information board and a nearby statue to David Lloyd George, the town's former Liberal MP and minister, then turn LEFT beneath the castle down to toilets. *The metal balcony jutting out from the castle was where Prince Charles greeted the crowds after his controversial investiture as Prince of Wales in 1969.* Continue down to the car park entrance – *to the left is the Harbour Trust Office 1840* – and on to the quay overlooking the river Seiont and small harbour. Turn RIGHT, taking care not to trip over any mooring chains, to pass an information board on the former Slate Quay. Go across the Aber swing bridge – *built across the river's mouth in 1974*. Turn LEFT for a classic view across the river to the castle. Return across the bridge and turn LEFT to pass the gated town entrance. Go past The Anglesey pub and along the promenade beneath the town walls – *with a good view across to Anglesey* – soon passing through the arch of Porth-yr-Aur (Golden Gate). At the corner of the town walls you will see the rare Jesse window of St Mary's church – *incorporated into the walls as the garrison church in 1307 and extensively renovated in the early 19thC*. Continue along the promenade, past the nearby Sailing Club.

2 At bollards turn sharp RIGHT then go along the end of Victoria Dock and past the Maritime Museum. *Victoria Dock was built in the 1870s in response to the demands of the slate industry, but later went into decline. After a regeneration programme the dock has become a marina and land developed into a fashionable part of Caernarfon to live and visit, with restaurants, hotels and apartments.* Turn LEFT on the signposted Lôn Las Menai alongside the marina soon crossing a footbridge over a wide slipway – *used to pull boats out of the water for repairs, and which pre-dates the dock*. Go past the Galeri and at the dock's corner turn LEFT past the modern complex to the promenade. Follow it RIGHT – *with good views along the Menai Strait*.

26

WALK 15

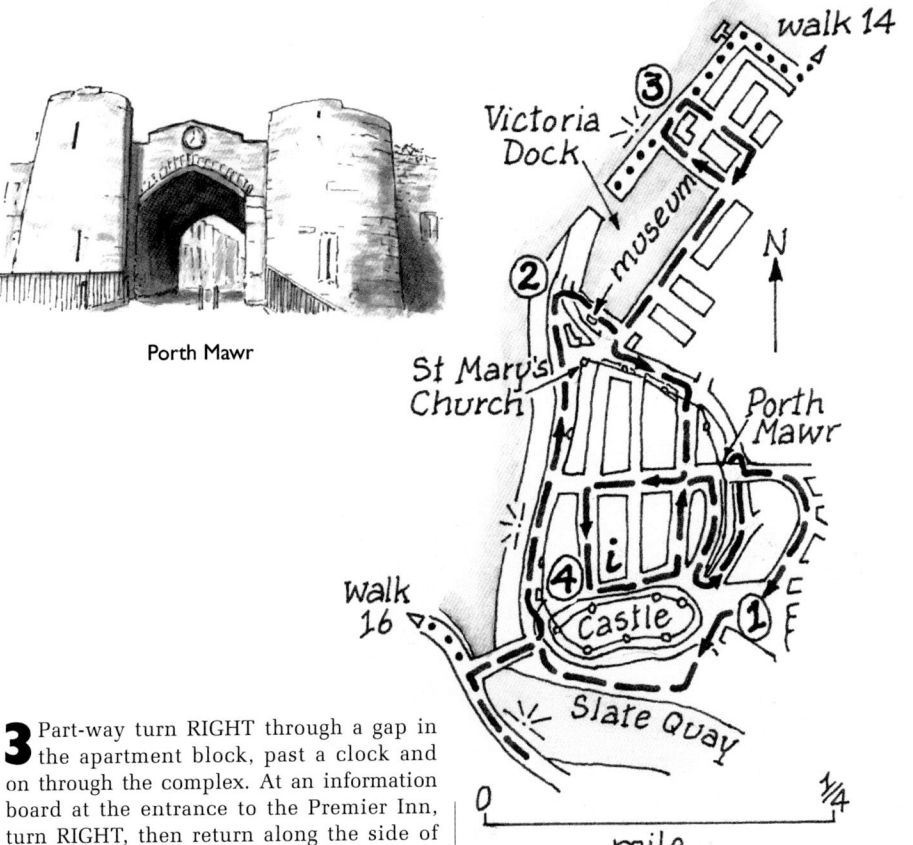

Porth Mawr

3 Part-way turn RIGHT through a gap in the apartment block, past a clock and on through the complex. At an information board at the entrance to the Premier Inn, turn RIGHT, then return along the side of the Victoria Dock to the road by the anchor. Turn LEFT and continue along the pavement beside the impressive outer walls, then turn RIGHT through the next but one archway – *added in the 19thC to improve access* – into the old walled town. Continue up Northgate Street – *once a street of notoriety for sailors visiting the port (see the plaque on the wall of the 16thC Black Boy Inn)*. At crossroads turn RIGHT along High Street – *the old town's traditional business centre* – then LEFT up Shirehall Street, passing Gwynedd Council buildings incorporating the town's former jail. *At the junction to the right is the columned frontage of County Hall. Dating from the 1860s and now the County Court, it stands on the site of earlier Shire Houses.*

4 Turn LEFT past the Information Centre and entrance to the castle, then LEFT down Palace Street – *once boasting 15 inns* – past the old Market Hall (1832). At crossroads turn RIGHT and just before Porth Mawr (Great Gate) – *for centuries the only entrance to the town, accessed by a drawbridge, which was closed during a nightly curfew* – turn RIGHT along Hole-in-the Wall Street, past an information board and on beneath the town walls, containing the remains of the Bell Tower. Turn LEFT, then LEFT again down the next road beneath the outer town walls to Tal-y-Bont arch. *To your right are the small window and door of a tiny room, once a jail and now used as a chapel.* Go under the arch and up steps to your right. Now turn LEFT along Eastgate Street to Turf Square – *for centuries the site of the town stocks.* At crossroads turn RIGHT to reach Castle Square.

WALK 16
ST BAGLAN'S CHURCH

DESCRIPTION A 6 mile walk exploring the coast and countryside immediately west of Caernarfon, with extensive coastal views. From the historic walled town the route follows a scenic minor road along the edge of the Menai Strait – a section of the new Wales Coast Path. It then heads east past a remote ancient church on field paths and quiet country roads to Bontnewydd, where it joins the Lôn Eifion recreational trail for a return alongside the Welsh Highland narrow gauge steam railway. Allow about 3 hours.
START Castle Square, Caernarfon [SH 479626].

1 From the statue of Sir Hugh Owen, a leading educationalist, head towards the Castle, past an information board and a nearby statue to David Lloyd George, the town's former Liberal MP and minister, then turn LEFT beneath the castle down to toilets. *The metal balcony jutting out from the castle was where Prince Charles greeted the crowds after his controversial investiture as Prince of Wales in 1969.* Cross to the other side and continue beneath the imposing castle (See Walk 15 for information) past seats, then cross Aber swing bridge over the mouth of the river Seiont. *Ferries operated here until 1900 when a road bridge was built. In 1974 it was replaced with Aber bridge which swings open to allow boats to pass through.* Turn RIGHT along the pavement overlooking the shore – *with a good view looking back at the castle and town walls* – then continue on the minor road along the edge of the Menai Strait – *enjoying good views across to nearby Anglesey*. Later you pass the Royal Town Golf Club, then a slipway for boats – *enjoying good views inland of the mountains of Snowdonia*. Ahead is the narrow western entrance to the Menai Strait. After passing Tŷ Calch – *another boat launching area using tractors* – the road continues south into the Gwyrfai estuary and Foryd Bay. *The sand and mud exposed at low tide provide an important habit for native and overwintering birds.*

2 Soon after passing Cynifryn take a signposted path through a kissing gate and go across the field to the left-hand side of the walled enclosed small ancient church of St Baglan. *This small church, dating from the 13thC, stands on the site of an earlier church. It is a rare example of a medieval church not restored during the 19thC and therefore containing its original 18thC furnishings, resulting in it being Grade 1 listed by Cadw. It is now owned by the Friends of Friendless Churches charity and looked after by local people.* Continue across the field to a ladder-stile, then follow the hedge along the next field to a kissing gate. Continue along the edge of another field towards a house, soon rising past nearby outbuildings to a gap in the hedge ahead. Pass above the house, through another boundary gap and go down the field to a ladder-stile to join the house's access track, which takes you to a road. Turn RIGHT and follow this quiet country road to crossroads. Go along the road ahead, signposted to Y Bontnewydd, past houses, later alongside the river Gwyrfai.

3 After passing under a railway bridge on the outskirts of Bontnewydd, turn LEFT through a gate and follow the wide surfaced Lôn Eifion link path up to cross the narrow gauge Welsh Highland railway line via gates to join the recreational route for walkers and cyclists at Bontnewydd Halt. Now simply follow it north beside the railway – *if timed well enjoying close views of the steam locomotive hauled trains. Both Lôn Eifion and the railway share the trackbed of the former Caernarfon-Afonwen standard gauge railway (1867-1964). The 3 mile section between Caernarfon and Dinas was the first section of the narrow gauge railway to be opened in 1997.* After 1¾ miles you emerge from the tree-lined route at a good viewpoint along the river to Caernarfon castle. Lôn Eifion continues beside the road to the railway's booking office and shop. Cross the nearby high footbridge over the railway and turn LEFT along the road to enter the corner of Castle Square.

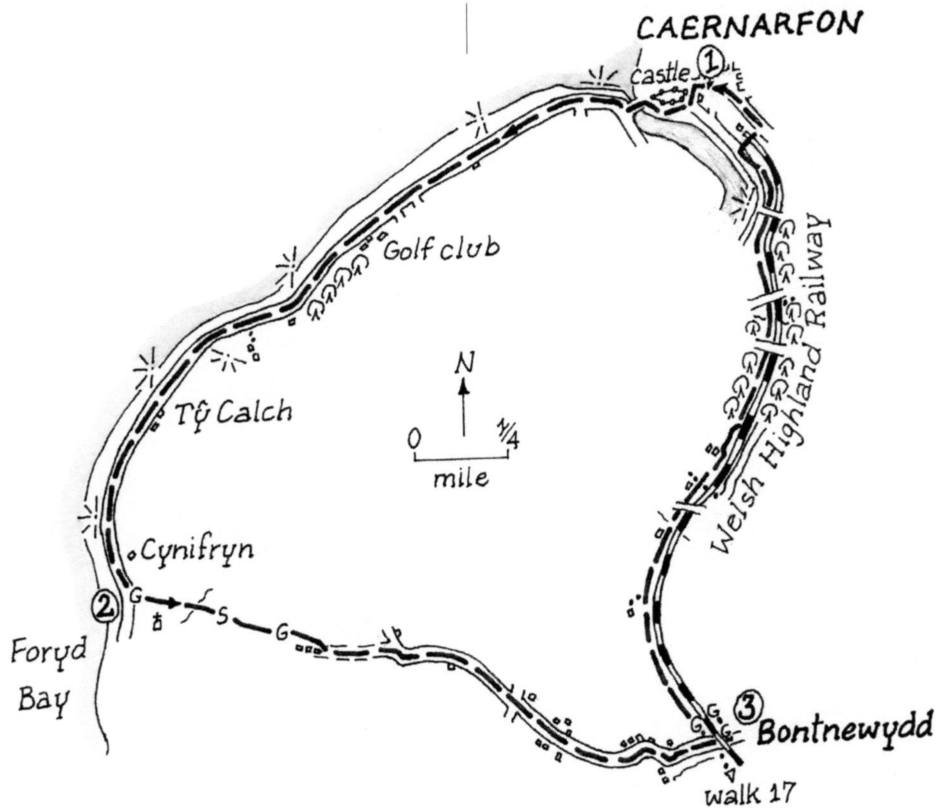

WALK 16

St Baglan's Church

WALK 17
WELSH HIGHLAND RAILWAY

DESCRIPTION A 7 mile walk exploring the countryside between Rhostryfan and Bontnewydd, which, if timed right, offers opportunities for close views of steam trains on the Welsh Highland Railway. The walk Incorporates three different recreational routes: a new Slate Trail footpath on the former Bryngwyn Branch narrow gauge railway (See Walk 18) at the beginning and end, the Lôn Gwyrfa trail, and from Bontnewydd, the Lôn Eifion trail alongside the Welsh Highland Railway. Allow about 3½ hours.

START Old railway station site car park, Rhostryfan [SH 498579].

DIRECTIONS Just south of Bontnewydd turn off the A487 and follow a road to Rhostryfan. At minor crossroads by a shop turn left and follow the road round past a school to find the car park at its end.

The Welsh Highland Railway, using powerful narrow gauge steam locomotives, offers a spectacular 25 mile journey from Caernarfon through the heart of Snowdonia to Porthmadog. It owes its origins to several separate narrow gauge railway initiatives during the 19th and early 20thC, primarily to serve local slate quarries. In 1922 the Welsh Highland Railway was formed from the merger of two companies and work began to construct missing links, which enabled the opening of a narrow gauge railway between Dinas, just south of Caernarfon, to Porthmadog in 1923. It faced difficulties from the beginning. The slate industry was in decline and passenger traffic was competing with new road transport. The Ffestiniog Railway took over its management in 1934 but by 1937 all traffic had ceased. Most of the railway was dismantled during World War II. However the trackbed remained and there began a long and controversial campaign to restore the railway and extend it to Caernarfon. Eventually the Ffestiniog Railway Company took responsibility for the restoration and after much voluntary effort and grant funding, the line was completed in 2011.

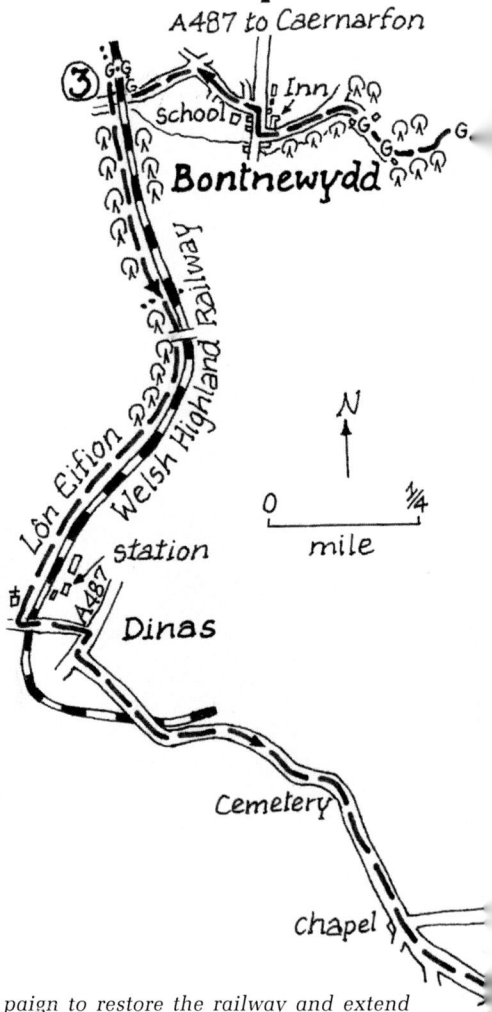

1 Follow the wide Slate Trail north, later tree-lined and passing under a bridge, to a road by Tryfan crossing on the Welsh Highland railway. Cross the railway and follow the narrow access road near it. After passing a bridge over the railway, the road descends and bends north to end at Gwredog Isaf. Follow a rough track to a gate by a ruin

WALK 17

and along the top of a small wooded valley, gradually descending to cross a bridge over the river. Go up the narrow lane, then at a junction by a house turn LEFT to a gate. Now follow the enclosed surfaced Lon Gwyrfa trail west to Plas Glan Yr Afon, then a rough track through the farm. Go along its access track, past a nearby house. The track becomes lined by high hedges.

2 Go through a waymarked gate on the left opposite an old iron gate. Angle LEFT across the field and on through a waymarked gate. Turn RIGHT along the field edge to a ladder-stile. Go up the next large field, then at the fence turn LEFT to cross a ladder-stile in the corner and an old iron ladder-stile ahead. Go along the field edge to another ladder-stile, then follow a path between boundaries and past an old iron gate. Continue between a wall and a tree boundary (can get overgrown in summer) to a kissing gate, then between walls to another kissing gate. Follow the large wall to a gate, then an enclosed path, soon descending to an iron gate by a house. Follow the path above the river to a house at Dol Pandy Farm. Go past Pandy Bach ahead and up the access lane to a road. Follow it above the river to The Newborough Arms in Bontnewydd. Turn RIGHT along the main road, past an imposing church, then cross with care to a road opposite on the signposted Lôn Eifion. Follow the road past the school and out of the village. Just before a bridge, follow the signposted Lôn Eifion up to cross the Welsh Highland Railway by Bontnewydd Halt.

3 Follow the wide surfaced route south alongside the railway for 1 mile, later mature tree-lined and passing under a high bridge, to Dinas station. *Both follow a section of the former Caernarfon-Afonwen standard gauge railway (1867-1964). At Dinas Junction, as it was known, slate carried from the Moel Tryfan quarries by the North Wales Narrow Gauge Railway was transferred onto the mainline railway for taking to Caernarfon.* Just before a bridge go through a gap and up steps onto the road bridge. Follow the road to the A487. *Dinas village, with its former coaching inns, developed on turnpike roads.* Turn RIGHT then go along a minor road opposite signposted to Rhos Isaf/Rhostryfan. Shortly it crosses the Welsh Highland Railway then continues past a cemetery. At crossroads by an old chapel follow the road straight ahead through the small community. At a junction turn LEFT up the narrow road. At the next junction turn LEFT then RIGHT up another narrow road for ¼ mile.

4 On the bend by Bryn Elen go through the kissing gate ahead and past the end of the house to a small gate. Go up the field to steps and a small gate in the corner. Go up the left edge of rough upland pasture, then an area of scrub and gorse, and on up to join the former Bryngwyn Branch line. Go through the kissing gate and follow the signposted Slate Trail path along the former trackbed, across two minor roads to the main road in Rhostryfan, then along a wide stony path, under a bridge, to the start.

WALK 18
BRYNGWYN BRANCH LINE

DESCRIPTION A 3¼ mile walk exploring the elevated countryside south of Rhostryfan, featuring a delightful recently created path on a section of a former narrow gauge railway, an old incline that linked upland slate quarries with the railway, and good views. Allow about 2 hours.
START Old railway station site car park, Rhostryfan [SH 498579].
DIRECTIONS See Walk 17.

In 1877 the North Wales Narrow Gauge Railway Company opened a branch line via Rhostryfan to Bryngwyn to service slate quarries on the Moel Tryfan plateau. As well as slate and local supplies, it also carried passengers until 1913. Slate transportation then gradually declined and the line closed in 1937.

1 Cross a footbridge over a nearby stream and go through a small gate opposite. Follow the wide slate surfaced railway path to the main road, then go through the kissing gate by an information board opposite. Now follow the kissing gated railway path south for just over 1 mile across two minor roads, then along the former trackbed through attractive countryside, later passing Cae Haidd, to its end at a minor road. Turn LEFT up the road, past a house, then under power cables – *with views ahead of Moel Tryfan and its slate quarries*. After a cattle grid take a signposted path between Bryn Helen (near the site of the former Bryngwyn station) and a stone cottage to a footbridge over a stream. Follow the path up to a kissing gate, and across reedy gorse covered ground up to a road junction by Bryn chapel. Turn LEFT and just before a bridge over a stream turn RIGHT to follow a path up the former incline across Open Access land. *The double track incline went up to Drumhead, where it connected with tramways from the quarries.* At a crossroad of paths by cottages, turn LEFT, taking the path's left fork across gorse covered terrain. After crossing a stream, take the path's left fork across the slope to a minor road.

2 Take a signposted path along the stony access track opposite (Cae Haidd Bach). After ¼ mile go through a kissing gate by a cattle grid. Go up the right hand field edge past another kissing gate, then angle away from the boundary across the tussocky ground to pass under power cables to a kissing gate in a boundary corner. Cross the next field corner to another kissing gate. Continue down a large field to pass between walls near the corner to a gate by Hafotty Newydd farm. Go along the enclosed path past the house, then turn LEFT through a nearby gate, and RIGHT along the farm's access track. After about 100 yards turn LEFT past a small waymark post at a nearby wall corner. Continue near the wall to a kissing gate, then follow the path down to the right hand wall corner. Turn RIGHT between boundaries to go through a small iron gate on the left. Pass beneath the farm building, descend steps then the field to a stile/gate onto the farm's access track. Follow it down to a minor road. Go down the narrow left fork ahead to rejoin your outward route.

WALK 18 & 19

WALK 19
MOEL SMYTHO

DESCRIPTION A ¾ mile walk around part of Uwchgwyrfai Common, associated with famous Welsh author Dr Kate Roberts, whose local museum can be visited (*open Tue–Fri 10.00–16.00, Sat & Sun 12.00–16.00. Closed Winter. Charge*). The walk features a delightful old quarry tramway on the northern slopes of Moel Tryfan and the small hill of Moel Smytho (1125 ft/343 metres), both offering panoramic views. Allow about 2½ hours.

START Minor junction above Rhosgadfan [SH 511571] or car parking area at Braich Moel Smytho [SH 584615].

DIRECTIONS On entering Rhosgadfan turn left up a road signposted to Waenfawr/Cae'r Gors, past the Kate Roberts museum to crossroads by Capel Rhosgadfan. (For the alternative start turn left and follow the road as shown.) Go up the road ahead to a junction just beyond a cattle grid. Here are off-road parking places.

1 At the nearby bend take a path to the left of a stony access track across the common up to a crossroad of paths. Follow the wide path ahead past a wall and up to join a narrow stony track – *a 2 mile long narrow gauge tramway, built in 1876, to transport slate by wagons behind steam locomotives from Alexandra quarry on Moel Tryfan to the Bryngwyn branch line and on to Caernarfon.* Follow it LEFT, rising gently – *enjoying extensive views*. At tips turn sharp LEFT to follow a path down to a wall corner – *with a good view to Snowdon* – and on down to join an access track. Just after crossing the stream turn RIGHT to follow a wide path across the common, over a crosspath, to a path T-junction by the forest Follow it LEFT near the wall. Soon after passing a ladder-stile/gate take a stony path angling LEFT up the heather covered slope of Moel Smytho to a large boulder on its summit. The path now makes a steady descent across its northern slopes to a wall corner. Keep ahead beside the wall, then at its next corner follow a wide path angling RIGHT. After joining another wide path continue beside the wall, soon joining Penrallt's access track, then turn LEFT up another track to join the nearby road to reach the alternative parking area.

2 Go up a concrete then stony track. When it splits continue ahead along the concrete track. As it bends towards a cottage, follow a rough green track ahead a few yards, then angle RIGHT to reach an interesting information panel on the Uwchgwyrfai Common quarries. Follow a wide path leading away between walled enclosures, soon bending right and continuing down across the common to a walled enclosure. Follow a narrow path beside the wall, then at its corner bear LEFT up a path to join a nearby house's access track. Follow it to cottages then continue along a scenic narrow upland road to the junction.

WALK 20
MOEL TRYFAN

DESCRIPTION A 5 mile walk around Moel Tryfan (1400 ft/427 metres) and its slate quarries. The route rises to the foot of Moel Tryfan, offering an early opportunity for an optional short there and back climb to its summit. It continues south to the former Braich quarry, then heads north on tracks to pass above the huge quarry beneath Moel Tryfan's summit. It then follows a delightful former tramway on a gentle descent around Moel Tryfan's northern slopes, offering panoramic views. Allow about 3½ hours. The walk can be shortened by starting at a minor junction above Rhosgadfan [SH 511571]. (See Walk 19.)
START Crossroads by Capel Rhosgadfan [SH 508572].
DIRECTIONS On entering Rhosgadfan from Rhostryfan turn left up a road signposted to Waenfawr/Cae'r Gors, past the Kate Roberts museum to crossroads by Capel Rhosgadfan, where there is roadside parking.

*W*hilst other slate quarries in the area developed quickly during the 19thC, the upland quarries on the Moel Tryfan plateau were initially restricted by isolation, transportation problems and disputes. This all changed with the opening of the Bryngwyn branch of the North Wales Narrow Gauge Railway in 1877. Slate from the quarries was moved to Drumhead and down an incline to Bryngwyn station, then taken by rail to Dinas, where it was transferred onto the LNWR line for its journey to Caernarfon for shipping far and wide.

1 Go up the road, then take a signposted path opposite Bryn Teg. Go a few yards along a track then angle LEFT to a kissing gate. Follow the path to another kissing gate then up alongside a stream to a minor road. Follow it RIGHT then go up a narrow road on the left towards Moel Tryfan to join another. At its end by the cemetery turn LEFT then RIGHT at the wall corner up a green track towards a slate tip. Bend LEFT beneath its base to join a rough stony track, which rises past the side of the tip. At a crossroad of tracks beneath Moel Tryfan turn RIGHT along the former Alexandra quarry tramway through a short cutting. After passing through a wall, and just before the tramway becomes enclosed by walls turn RIGHT. (For Moel Tryfan summit turn left then follow a visible path rising up the hillside.)

2 Follow a path down past a house to a kissing gate. Pass between the house and a cottage, then turn RIGHT to follow a stony access track to a road. Follow it LEFT then take a signposted path down an access track past a ruin to its end, then follow a path beside a fence past a cottage and on through a gate ahead. Follow the enclosed path to a kissing gate, then go past the front of a cottage and on to a gate beneath tips. Follow its access track to a road. Turn LEFT along the grass verge past a side road. Shortly, at a grid road sign turn LEFT on a signposted path along an access track. After about 40 yards take a path angling RIGHT to cross a small bridge over a stream. Go along the field edge to a small gate in the corner. At the small field corner ahead turn LEFT up to a small makeshift gate, then continue up between walls to an iron gate. Go up beside the wall and at its corner follow a path up the next field, through a gap in a low wall and on up beneath tips to a wall gap and onto the rise above. Descend then turn RIGHT between the wall and an embankment of slate waste. At a fenced-off archway in it, climb onto the embankment and descend steps to a small gate at the other side of the archway. Go through another nearby archway and on past Bryn Glas cottage. Follow the path ahead beside the wall to a kissing gate/gate, then continue along the walled path.

3 At its end turn LEFT along a stony access track. When it bends left continue along a lesser track ahead, then follow an enclosed path up past the large water filled former Braich slate quarry (1833 -1914). Continue with a path beside the wall by a large house. At the wall corner by a red topped post – *with a good view of the Nantlle ridge* – follow a path angling LEFT to a nearby single story cottage. Ignore the stony track but

WALK 20

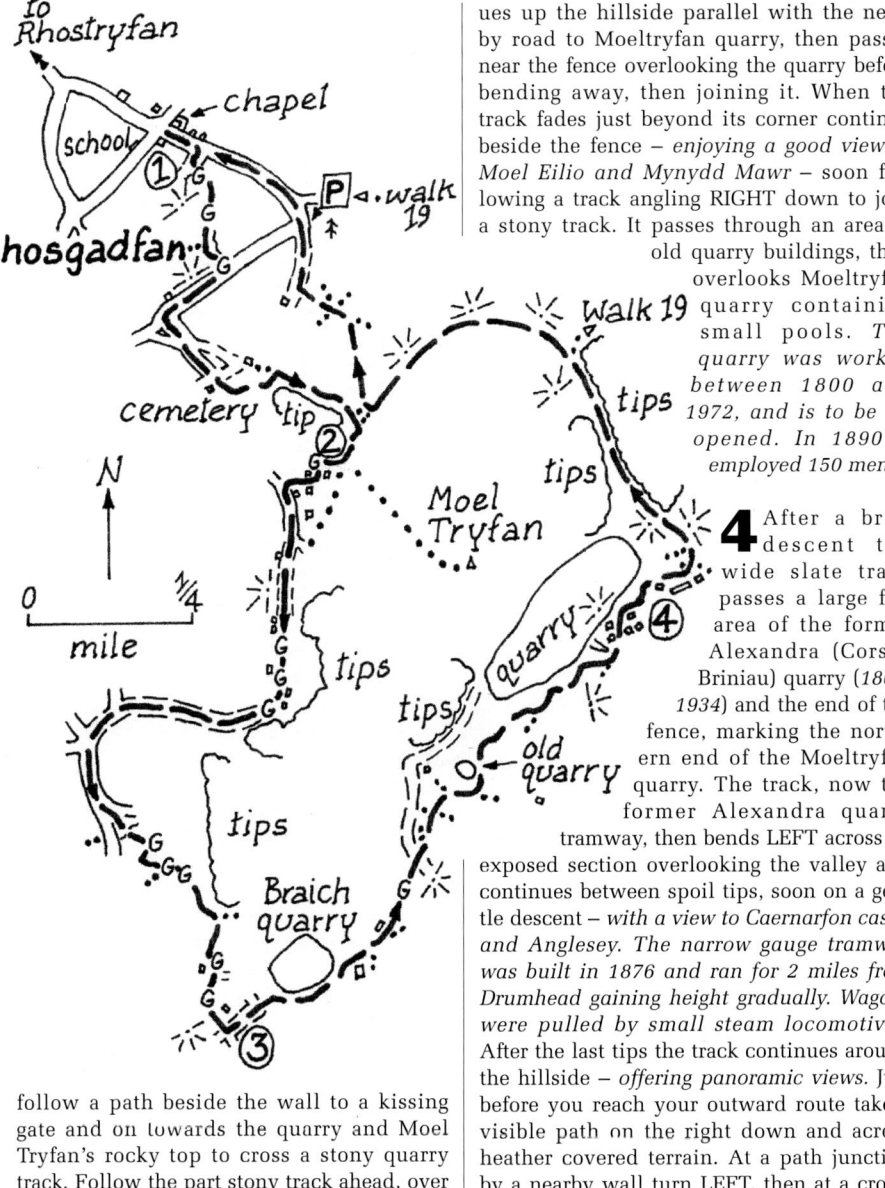

ues up the hillside parallel with the nearby road to Moeltryfan quarry, then passes near the fence overlooking the quarry before bending away, then joining it. When the track fades just beyond its corner continue beside the fence – *enjoying a good view of Moel Eilio and Mynydd Mawr* – soon following a track angling RIGHT down to join a stony track. It passes through an area of old quarry buildings, then overlooks Moeltryfan quarry containing small pools. *The quarry was worked between 1800 and 1972, and is to be reopened. In 1890 it employed 150 men.*

4 After a brief descent the wide slate track passes a large flat area of the former Alexandra (Cors y Briniau) quarry (*1862-1934*) and the end of the fence, marking the northern end of the Moeltryfan quarry. The track, now the former Alexandra quarry tramway, then bends LEFT across an exposed section overlooking the valley and continues between spoil tips, soon on a gentle descent – *with a view to Caernarfon castle and Anglesey. The narrow gauge tramway was built in 1876 and ran for 2 miles from Drumhead gaining height gradually. Wagons were pulled by small steam locomotives.* After the last tips the track continues around the hillside – *offering panoramic views.* Just before you reach your outward route take a visible path on the right down and across heather covered terrain. At a path junction by a nearby wall turn LEFT, then at a crossroad of paths keep ahead, taking the narrower left fork down to a stony access track near a house. Follow it down to the bend of the road, which takes you down to the start.

follow a path beside the wall to a kissing gate and on towards the quarry and Moel Tryfan's rocky top to cross a stony quarry track. Follow the part stony track ahead, over a cross track, soon angling RIGHT to meet another stony cross track just before a small fenced off quarry. Follow it RIGHT briefly, then turn LEFT to follow a green track up past the fenced-off quarry. The track contin-

WALK 21
MYNYDD Y CILGWYN

DESCRIPTION A 5¼ mile (**A**), featuring the small hill of Mynydd y Cilgwyn (1138 feet/347 metres), the relics of Uwchgwyrfai Common and Nantlle valley's slate quarries, and good changing views throughout. Allow about 3½ hours. An alternative 4¾ mile (**B**) walk skirting Mynydd y Cilgwyn is included. For information on quarrying in the Nantlle valley see Walk 22.
START Talysarn [SH 492532].
DIRECTIONS See Walk 22.

1 Return to the road junction and turn right along Ffordd Nantle. At a mini roundabout turn LEFT and follow a stony track up the hillside, levelling out at a track junction. Keep ahead then go up a short track beneath a house, then a path between gorse and the garden boundary to a kissing gate. Follow the path up beside a low wall, then through bracken and gorse to a stony track. Turn LEFT then after 10 yards follow a path leading RIGHT from a red topped post through gorse to a kissing gate. The path soon rises through gorse and bracken then across a field. Go through a wall gap and on to a kissing gate at the end of a short section of wall at a crossroad of paths. Go up the short section of walled path, and on up to another kissing gate by a ruin. Continue up the path, past a kissing gate, then up between walls to another kissing gate. Go up a nearby narrow walled path to a kissing gate. and through the slate arch of an old tramway ahead. Continue beside a road to a junction. Turn RIGHT along the narrow road on a signposted path to Y Fron

2 On its bend by a cottage and a converted chapel you have a choice. For **Walk A** follow a path ahead near a wall, past a telegraph pole and on up the southern heather/bilberry slopes of Mynydd y Cilgwyn to a low circle of stones on its summit – *offering extensive views. A nearby plaque marks the site of 7thC St Twrog's church.* Continue on a clear path across the top, Shortly the path bends north west then steadily descends to a stony cross-path just before a road. Follow it RIGHT, then turn RIGHT along a track. After passing through a fence the track steadily descends to a crossroad of tracks to join Walk B. Turn LEFT. For **Walk B** turn RIGHT along a stony track past a ruin and down its right fork. When it bends through a gate keep ahead down a path near the wall to the boundary of a landfill site – *part of the former Cilgwyn quarry, the oldest in the area which closed in 1965.* Turn LEFT up alongside the fence, past ruins and on up between the fence and a wall. Follow the wall up to a red topped post at its corner. Turn RIGHT along a cross path to join the stony track just above – *a former tramway that carried slate from nearby Cilgwyn quarry.* After an interesting information board on the local Uwchgwyrfai Common quarries continue with the tramway to join Walk A at a crossroad of tracks. Keep ahead.

3 Follow the track then a road to crossroads at Y Fron. Turn RIGHT, then go down a no through road (Tan y Fron/ Bron Eryri). At its end go through a kissing gate and along a rough track. Just before a fenced off area turn RIGHT and follow a faint green track down to a kissing gate/gate and on down between ruins. After a stream and an iron ladder-stile, the track bends south, passes through a gateway and descends to a kissing gate. Go through another one ahead and across the field to a ladder-stile. Follow a path ahead across reedy/ bracken covered terrain to a ladder-stile near a small ruin. Beyond reeds angle RIGHT to follow a path down into the valley, briefly joining a slate fence beneath tips, before continuing to the road in Nantlle. Turn RIGHT through the village.

4 Just past a bus stop turn RIGHT along a side road (Glan Rhonwy) and past Y Barics industrial workshops, Continue along Tai Nantlle past terraced cottages, then slate tips. Just past Bryn Deulyn, the road becomes a stony track and enters the slate quarry. The track passes between waste tips, then the substantial supports of a former tram-

WALK 21

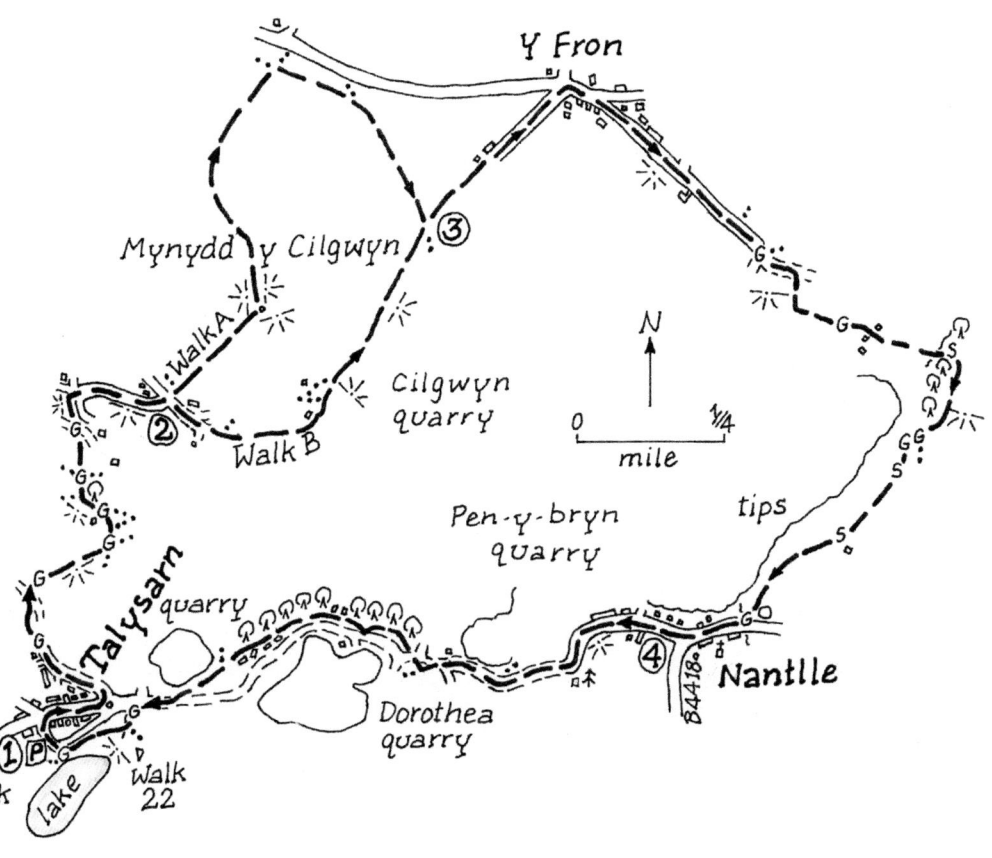

way, with hidden Pen-y-bryn quarry nearby, which closed in 1950. It then bends to the left of a slate structure. About 10 yards further, go half-LEFT on a path through trees, passing between large slate supports. Just beyond, take the right fork of the former tramway through a cutting, then under a bridge. Continue beside a substantial wall and through another cutting to emerge into an open area by the main track. *Just beyond a ruined quarry building is the large water-filled Dorothea quarry (1820-1970), popular with divers, despite claiming many lives.* A few yards before two metal posts where the main track begins to rise, look for a path through trees on the right (it may be overgrown but persevere). After 10 yards a wide path continues through a rock cutting, then with a tunnel ahead, bends half-left between walls to pass old quarry buildings. The path then continues through a more open area, joins a green track and passes another substantial water-filled quarry to join the main stony track. A few yards after another track rising right, pass between two large boulders on the left to a kissing gate. Turn RIGHT on the waymarked path then RIGHT again across a footbridge. Follow the path – *with a good view of a nearby lake* – to a kissing gate behind a seat onto an access road, which you follow LEFT to the nearby car park.

WALK 22
CWM LLYFNI

DESCRIPTION A varied 4¾ mile (**A**) or 4¼ mile (**B**) walk exploring a valley near Talysarn, featuring a local community recreational area, lake, attractive river, old slate quarries and good views of Snowdon. Allow about 3 hours.
START Talysarn [SH 492532].
DIRECTIONS From Caernarfon follow the A487 south, then turn off for Penygroes. In the village take the B4418 to Talysarn. At the T-junction turn left, then right at a monument to Robert Williams Parry – one of Wales most renowned poets (1884-1956). At a 30 mph sign/ no through road ahead, turn right into a small car parking area..

*F*rom the early 19thC the Nantlle valley became an important slate quarrying area, boosted by the opening in 1828 of the horse-drawn Nantlle narrow gauge (3ft 6in) railway which enabled slate to be transported from the quarries to Caernarfon for shipping far and wide. In 1965 it became part of the Caernarvonshire Railway and by 1872 the line from Talysarn to Caernarfon had been converted to a standard gauge railway run by steam locomotives. The remainder of the line continued as a horse-drawn tramway connecting local quarries with transhipment facilities at Talysarn. Horses continued to be used under LNWR and later British Rail ownership until just before the railway was closed in 1963. The method of quarrying was to dig down, creating large deep pits, which were subject to flooding. During the 19thC to help alleviate the problem a lake in the valley was gradually drained and in 1895 the Afon Llyfni was realigned and canalised.

1 Go along the adjoining minor road and on the bend go through a kissing gate. Turn LEFT along a path overlooking a lake – with a good view of the Nantlle ridge and Snowdon beyond. Cross a footbridge over a stream and take the path heading half-RIGHT across the hillside past seats, shortly descending to pass the end of the lake and cross its outflow. Continue with the path to a small gate and a path junction, (The one ahead returns to the start). Turn LEFT to join a narrow surfaced path which you follow LEFT, later passing two side paths to descend steps to a road. Follow the signposted path opposite through trees, across a footbridge over a stream and a larger one over the Afon Llyfni to a kissing gate – *enjoying a good view along the river to Snowdon*. Follow the path ahead past an area of gorse and across reedy terrain to a kissing gate onto a road by Tanyrallt chapel. For **Walk B** go up the track opposite to point 3.)

2 Turn LEFT along the road – *with a good view across to Talysarn* – passing beneath slate waste tips. After passing a 30 mph sign and a house go through a kissing gate on the right amongst trees. Follow the path alongside the stream up to a kissing gate, and on to another kissing gate to cross a footbridge over the stream. Go along the right hand field edge, passing above a large quarry to a kissing gate. Continue ahead across quarry waste, down slate steps and on along the field edge to a kissing gate/gate onto an access track by a cottage. Follow it LEFT.

3 Shortly go through a kissing gate on the right. Follow a narrow green track up between spoil heaps and past one on the left, then go past a red topped post to follow a path ahead, initially below the track, then past ruined quarry buildings. The delightful raised path – *offering good views across Cardigan Bay and to Holyhead Mountain* – then passes a huge water filled quarry, before continuing along a field edge, through a gap in a hedge and on to a kissing gate by a stream. The path continues by a wall to another kissing gate onto a minor road. Follow it down – *with a good view along the coast to Anglesey* – to a junction. Turn LEFT.

4 Just past Tyn Llwyn cottage take a signposted path through a gate. Go along the access track, then just after it bends at the second large pool go half-RIGHT on the waymarked path along a green track to a gate. Go past the house and across a sleeper

WALK 22

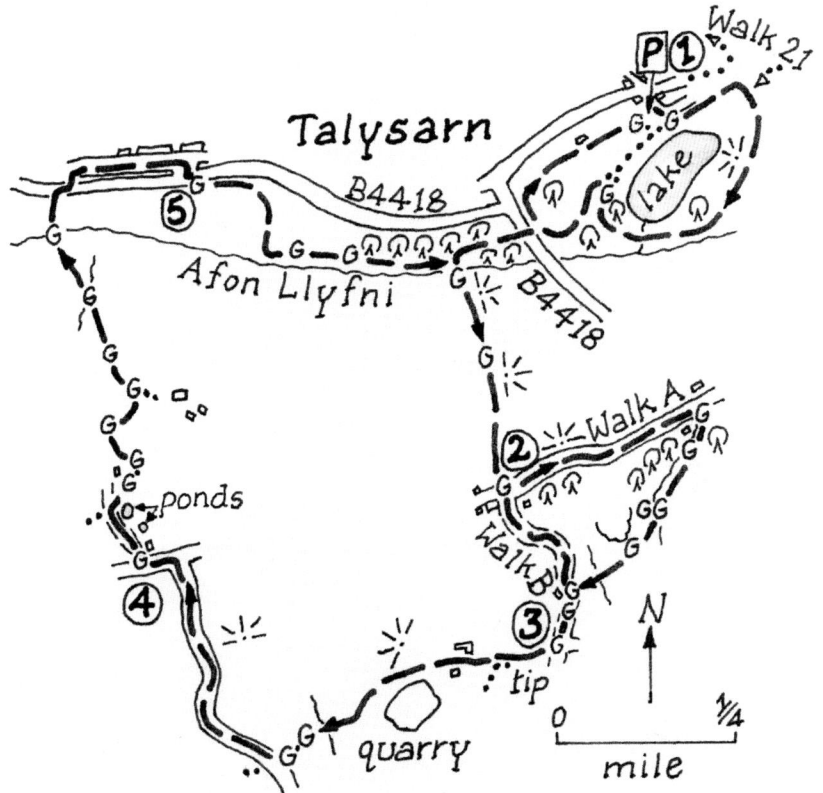

bridge over a stream to a small metal gate. Cross another sleeper bridge beyond, then turn LEFT then RIGHT along the field edge to cross a gate in the corner by a stream (or continue further round the field to a gateway). In the next field turn RIGHT and follow the boundary round to a small metal gate. Turn LEFT briefly along the edge of the next field then angle RIGHT across the corner to a kissing gate/gate and on across reedy terrain to a gated footbridge over the stream. Go across the middle of the large field to cross a large gated footbridge over the river Llyfni. Follow the enclosed path up to the road. Turn RIGHT along the grass verge into Talysarn, then go along the adjoining minor road (Hyfrydle) past houses, then return to the main road.

5 Continue briefly along the opposite grass verge to take a signposted path down to a kissing gate. Turn LEFT and follow a good path parallel with the wall and on by another low wall, after which the raised path bends to the river and the remains of an old bridge. Turn LEFT along the reedy river bank to a small iron gate. Continue alongside the attractive canalised river to a kissing gate, then beneath tree covered spoil heaps to join your outward route at the bridge over the river. Follow it to the road and into the park opposite. Take a path leading LEFT to the skate park, then turn RIGHT to follow the path past the football pitch, then a stony access track to a kissing gate to reach the car park beyond.

PRONUNCIATION

Welsh	English equivalent
c	always hard, as in **c**at
ch	as in the Scottish word lo**ch**
dd	as th in **th**en
f	as f in o**f**
ff	as ff in o**ff**
g	always hard, as in **g**ot
ll	no real equivalent. It is like 'th' in then, but with an 'L' sound added to it, giving 'thlan' for the pronunciation of the Welsh 'Llan'.

In Welsh the accent usually falls on the last-but-one syllable of a word.

KEY TO THE MAPS

- ➙ Walk route and direction
- ═ Metalled road
- ─ ─ ─ Unsurfaced road
- • • • • Footpath/route adjoining walk route
- ∿ River/stream
- ⚇ Trees
- ▬▬ Railway
- **G** Gate
- **S** Stile
- **F.B.** Footbridge
- ↘↙ Viewpoint
- **P** Parking
- **T** Telephone

THE COUNTRYSIDE CODE

- Be safe – plan ahead and follow any signs
- Leave gates and property as you find them
- Protect plants and animals, and take your litter home
- Keep dogs under close control
- Consider other people

Open Access
Some routes cross areas of land where walkers have the legal right of access under The CRoW Act 2000 introduced in May 2005. Access can be subject to restrictions and closure for land management or safety reasons for up to 28 days a year. Details from: www.naturalresourceswales.gov.uk. Please respect any notices.

Useful information
Gwynedd Council Rights of Way:
www.gwynedd.gov.uk or 01286 679536
Welsh Highland Railway: www.festrail.co.uk

About the author, David Berry

David is an experienced walker with a love of the countryside and an interest in local history. He is the author of a series of walks guidebooks covering North Wales, where he has lived and worked for many years, and been a freelance writer for Walking Wales magazine. He has also worked as a Rights of Way surveyor across North Wales and served as a member of Denbighshire Local Access Forum. For more information visit: www.davidberrywalks.co.uk

Published by **Kittiwake-Books Limited**
3 Glantwymyn Village Workshops, Glantwymyn, Machynlleth, Montgomeryshire SY20 8LY

© Text & map research: David Berry 2013
© Maps & illustrations: Kittiwake-Books Ltd 2013
Drawings by Morag Perrott
Cover photos: Main: View towards Penrhyn Quarry. Inset: Caernarfon Castle. David Berry

Care has been taken to be accurate. However neither the author nor the publisher can accept responsibility for any errors which may appear, or their consequences. If you are in any doubt about access, check before you proceed.

Printed by Mixam, UK.

ISBN: **978 1 908748 09 6**